C0057 13114

D1151243

Stosstrupptaktik

b
d

G
Li
n

STOSSTRUPPTAKTIK

GERMAN ASSAULT TROOPS OF THE

FIRST WORLD WAR
THE FIRST STORMTROOPERS

by

Stephen Bull

Glasgow Life Glasgow Libraries	
A	
C 005713114	
Askews & Holts	10-Sep-2014
940.41343 ⌣	£12.99

First published in 2007

Copyright © Stephen Bull 2007, 2014

ISBN 978-0-7509-5837-0

This edition published in Great Britain in 2014 by
Spellmount, an imprint of The History Press.
The Mill, Brimscombe Port, Stroud
Gloucestershire GL5 2QG
Website: www.spellmount.com

1 3 5 7 9 8 6 4 2

British Library Cataloguing in Publication Data:

A catalogue record for this book is available
from the British Library

The right of Stephen Bull to be identified
as the author of this work has been asserted by him
in accordance with the Copyright, Designs
and Patents Act 1988

All rights reserved. No part of this publication may be
reproduced, stored in a retrieval system or transmitted in
any form or by any means, electronic, mechanical,
photocopying, recording or otherwise,
without prior permission in writing from
Spellmount Limited, Publishers.

Front jacket: a field postcard by artists Sluyterman and Langwede. The question is – for which war was it created? Part of the argument of this book is that there is a traceable link from the *Stosstruppen* of World War I to the Stormtroopers of World War II.

Contents

Introduction

The infantry commander shouts *Drauf!*, and we rush forward. But where is the expected enemy fire? There is hardly any. His line is not so near as we thought and we had to run. I soon became out of breath and couldn't see out of the eye pieces of my gas mask so I tore it off. After all we thought this was going to be our last day; there isn't going to be any escape for us … There was a little machine gun fire and some of our chaps caught it. *Leutnant* Wiese was hit and the man carrying the explosive with me either fell over or was wounded … Then we reached the barbed wire, our objective. But there is nothing for us to do. The wire is completely destroyed. There wasn't really any trench left, just craters and craters. Now I looked back the way we had come and there was a swarm of men following, I couldn't stop a lump coming to my throat. Only a few of the enemy had survived the storm; some were wounded. They stood with their hands up.

Such was the experience of *Gefreiter* Paul Kretschmer of the 28th Pioneer Battalion on the morning of 21 March 1918: the opening of Operation Michael, the *Kaiserschlacht*, or Kaiser offensive. The men that followed the pioneers – ultimately seventy-six infantry assault and mobile divisons – attacked across a swathe of more than fifty miles of the Western Front, all the way from Arras in the north to La Fere in the south. Their aim was to break the front, and tear the British from their French Allies, in an attack which was designed as a precursor to further thrusts which might strike all the way to the sea, and end four long years of conflict. This was, in Ludendorff's words, 'an operation in which we could bring to bear the whole of our superiority', it was 'our great object'. If successful it could be a victory that would so shake Lloyd George and Clemenceau as to bring them to the peace table.

To many it would later seem as if the rule book of war had been torn up and thrown away. The advancing troops came on, not in lines, but small knots and strings, through the fog, gas and smoke, picking at the weakest parts of the defence. Light machine guns supported riflemen and grenadiers into the trench lines, and enemy posts were now hit from the flanks or rear. Flame-throwers and charges dealt with deeper bunkers; the remaining wire was blown or cut. Small mortars were carried forward to support platoons. Individual soldiers did not attempt to carry all their impedimenta in clumsy packs, but adopted assault gear with an emphasis on *Nahkampfmittel*, or the weapons of close combat. These 'Stormtroops' received orders from their officers, but frequently NCOs, even individual soldiers, were left to decide how best to carry them out. Fire served to keep the enemy heads down whilst comrades dashed forward – what would become known as 'fire and movement'. The first waves bypassed serious resistance, and where a major strong point was encountered the assault troops worked their way around. Like water forcing its way through a failing dam, the little trickles through tiny holes were followed by torrents – complete companies and battalions. Large bodies were now deployed to surround or destroy the demoralised men who found themselves trapped behind the German line. Artillery was deputed to respond directly to the needs of the attacking troops and not simply restricted to lengthy hammering.

Sometimes this seemed like some crazy exercise where the controlling hands had failed to remember to fix stop lines. This was no 'bite and hold': units often went on and on until they were stopped or could attack no more. Positions were not taken head-on but infiltrated. Reinforcements went not to the places where trouble was encountered, but to the points where resistance was at its weakest.

The overture to this Wagnerian performance was a furious five-hour bombardment played on 10,000 tubes of ordnance, 6,600 guns and 3,500 mortars. It was not a mindless cacophony, but a piece carefully orchestrated by *Oberst* Bruchmüller in seven movements. The first was 'surprise fire', with every heavy weapon opening up suddenly at 4.40 a.m., so as to catch the unwary out of cover, or without their gas masks at the ready. Like many good scores, the next passages were played more softly, squalls of shells creating curtains of whizzing steel to isolate reserves, or catch them where they concentrated. Some targets were purposely left unstruck, only to be deluged as soon as the men and guns stationed there attempted to intervene. At one Royal Artillery battery it was recorded that there had been almost no incoming fire for two hours, until at last they themselves started to shoot, and several accurate shells per minute were the immediate reply – counter-battery fire hampering the British gunners' attempts to support their infantry.

Though the barrage moved to a final crescendo, the last movement was more Strauss than Wagner: a teasing *Feuerwalze,* or creeping barrage, which rolled back and forth across the British positions. Men would take cover, the barrage would pass, men would emerge from their dugouts again and the shells would suddenly descend once more onto haplessly exposed targets. Yet the object of what was a fairly short bombardment by standards of the time was not merely to kill and maim; the shoots were planned to hit communication centres and command posts, to blind and dazzle the enemy ability to control. From behind this curtain the assault troops made their surprise entrance as quickly as possible, leaving dazed defenders no time to man their observation posts or machine guns.

By the end of the day many of the German units had advanced more than three miles. Just over two weeks later when the literal fog and the fog of war had both cleared, the extremity of the penetration at the juncture of the British and French forces was about forty miles, and a jagged rip of about fifty miles holed the old front line. By the standards of Napoleon these may not have been vast distances, but by the yardstick of the Western Front this was light speed – at Passchendaele, the third major battle of Ypres which had happened just six months earlier, the British and Canadians had crept forward at an average of about fifty metres per day. Now shells from the mightiest guns yet conceived, the *Wilhelmgeschütze,* screamed down on central Paris from a range of seventy miles, and some hundreds of French civilians would be killed. General Gough's enervated 5th Army had been thrown back not once, but several times, its tenuous foothold slipping and sliding under repeated blows. Gough was sacked.

Included in the 1,000 square miles of France that the German armies had captured was the old Somme battlefield of 1916 – a mere fragment of the territory which Hindenburg's men had now seized. This corner of the field had required of the British an hitherto unprecedented casualty bill to take in over four months of painful fighting, an attritional struggle which had shocked an otherwise stoic British public to the core. For a while it looked as though the German gamble might succeed. According to Field Marshal Douglas Haig's own account, French commander General Henri-Philippe Pétain, acclaimed victor of Verdun, now had the appearance of one 'in a funk' who had 'lost his nerve'. Even King George V showed signs of 'anxiety' during his visit to GHQ.

Such extraordinary events needed extraordinary explanations, and preferably ones that impugned the reputations of neither Allies nor the most senior British generals and politicians. Simple concepts were better still. Such explanations were soon found. Perhaps the most important of these was that the German 'Stormtroop tactics' had been developed in secret, on the Eastern Front, and had come as a surprise. Even those defeated in November 1918 would take solace in the myth of the Stormtrooper as symbolic of German will and determination in the face of overwhelming odds. According to the official version a step change in tactics had occured in March 1918, and no wonder then that there had been successes. The miracle was that the British were themselves able to adopt these 'new' methods quickly, turning them so effectively against their inventors just a few months later. Fifty years after the event it was still being claimed by some that the tactics which had apparently electrified the infantry battle were essentially the work of one man, General Oskar von Hutier (1857–1934), commander of the Eighteenth Army, whose cunning ruses had first been played out against Riga in September of the previous year.

Like all plausible misdirections, or partial understandings, the story of Stormtroop victory in March 1918 was based in truth. Yet the idea that shock tactics were some immaculate conception, and that ignorance and failure to think about the problems of the 'attack in position warfare' had dominated both sides of the line until that point, were complete fantasies. In fact, new tactical development had begun almost as soon as the old tactics had failed. The search for ways to break through the seemingly unassailable lines started as the first trenches were dug. Equally importantly, German theorists had not worked in a vacuum: ideas were tried out against French and British combatants, and both sides learned from their mistakes. New tactical manuals were written, and were captured and translated – sometimes very quickly. In some instances it is now difficult to determine whether a particular tactical concept was actually evolved by one side or the other. In any event the package that was the revolution in infantry combat came about little by little. In some cases the Germans established a short-lived lead, in others they did not.

Perhaps of almost equal importance was the misinterpretation of the Stormtrooper as one of the élite soldiers, to be regarded in an entirely different manner from the run-of-the-mill infantryman. Something of the sort happened: but it was never intended to be the case, the whole idea was to perfect tactics and teach them to all. Failure to train everyone to an equal standard resulted in the appearance of an élite – but by 1918 separate experimental units bearing a 'storm' designation were actually being reduced. Lastly there also appeared a fallacy – an extremely dangerous one – that somehow the new 'intelligent' tactics were less costly in terms of human life than the evils of 'stupid' trench warfare. In fact the reverse quickly proved to be true. As common sense would seem to have suggested, leaving the relative safety of holes in the ground to do battle with a determined foe was extremely perilous. Just as dangerous in fact as in 1914. This was not, however, something that anyone particularly cared to point out; either to recruits or to the public.

1
The Problem of Attack

The European powers may have had very different reasons for going to war in 1914, and many varied objectives, but when it came to their detailed expectations of battle and tactics these were surprisingly similar: the war would be short, and it would be won by the side which attacked most determinedly and persistently. The majority opinion in Germany was definitely that any war would be over quickly. After all, there were plenty of examples of wars since 1860 involving Germany, or German states, which had been very brief. The conclusion of these wars had usually been to the German advantage, and over the years, particularly under the guidance of the Iron Chancellor, Bismarck, war had been widely accepted as an instrument of policy.

The War of the Danish Duchies in 1864 lasted less than six months, and led to the occupation of Schleswig. Famously, the war in 1866 had been a 'seven weeks war'. It ended in Austria's total defeat, and the reining in of Hanover and other hitherto independent states in northern Germany, effectively adding five million people to the Prussian lands in the North German Confederation. The Franco-Prussian War was declared on 19 July 1870, and ended six months later with French capitulation. Paris had been besieged and Alsace and Lorraine seized for Prussia. At the same time the remaining independent states (most importantly Bavaria, Baden and Wurttemberg), were finally influenced to make King Wilhelm of Prussia, Emperor Wilhelm I of Germany. The Second Empire was declared at Versailles on 1 January 1871. The widespread conclusion for many patriotic Germans was that wars were usually quick, and in the longer term a good thing, despite short-term sacrifice.

Strangely, and despite his posturing and love of military uniforms and manoeuvres, Wilhelm II, who ascended the throne in 1888, would face stinging criticism declaring him a 'Peace Kaiser'.

Whilst the general expectation was of a short war, there were voices – surprisingly little heeded at the time – that suggested that any major European struggle between wealthy, heavily populated, and industrialised nations was likely to be both bloody and protracted. Some General Staff planners raised doubts: perhaps the war would not be won in a single campaign, or perhaps the artillery would be insufficient to deal with French and Belgian forts. There were also influential individuals who held contrary views. Amongst these were at least two who were extremely well placed to take an informed position: in Britain, Lord Kitchener, who immediately saw the war as a matter of 'years', rather than months; and in Germany, Helmuth von Moltke the younger, who was more pessimistic in private than his public face would suggest. In 1905, before he came to the pinnacle of his career as Chief of the General Staff, the brooding Moltke had even offered the surprising opinion that a general European war might be a war 'of murder'. Rather than agreeing with many of his contemporaries who prophesied that any conflict would be over in a year, he foresaw a 'people's war' which would turn into a 'long, difficult, painful struggle'. If anything, however, this percipience made him bend his efforts all the more towards finding a way to end the titanic struggle quickly. His calculation that reforms in both France and Russia would improve their military efficiency only added greater urgency to the need for a swift war – one that would be started soon. So it was that after 1906 Schlieffen's now infamous plan was not jettisoned, but modified, still with the major objective of finishing France as rapidly as possible.

There were even tacticians, albeit some of the more erudite theoretical school, who had begun to suggest the idea that weapons had advanced to the stage where present offensive tactics would be ineffective or unworkable. Though events would demonstrate that there was more than a grain of truth in this line of reasoning, none was to offer any definitive solution to the problem he had postulated. In such a vacuum it was scarcely surprising that relatively little investment was made in the development of radically new infantry tactics to meet situations which might, or might not, arise in the event of war. Nevertheless, there were certain practical matters which could be adjusted, and were considered at length long before 1914. Formations, for example, had been changed in the past, and history taught that judicial alterations could be efficacious.

Whether 'open' or 'closed' order formations were more suitable had been a debate which had been going on in the Prussian army even before Germany itself came into existence as a nation state. After the *Bruderkrieg* war of 1866 which pitted Prussia against Austria, there had been a move towards accepting that modern, rifled small arms had given a new advantage to the defence. There was therefore some questioning of the accepted adage that no war could be won without vigourous offensive action. It was, however, extremely hard to formulate new infantry tactics, not only against the background of an 'attack orthodoxy', but the very real problem that more dispersed formations meant more dispersed fire, and more difficult command. History seemed to suggest that although skirmishers could exact terrible casualties on formed bodies of troops, when it came to solid bodies closing on scattered skirmishers, the latter had no option but to retire, or be completely overwhelmed by the denser unit.

By the first battles of the Franco-Prussian war it had become usual to push more troops into the 'skirmish line' early in an action, but still this was regarded as a mere preliminary to the real fight. Only after August 1870 and the slaughterhouse of St Privat when the Prussian Guard lost 6,000 men in half an hour, was it finally determined that existing practice had to be seriously modified. So it was that many of the infantry actions in the later stages of the war relied on skirmish lines, rather than deeper formations, to carry the burden of the action. Moreover, full advantage was now taken of the fact that soldiers armed with breech loaders in general, and not just designated skirmishers, could fire from the prone position. Shooting when lying down offered the significant benefits that the shooter was a smaller target and more difficult to see. At the same time, having both elbows and the body on the ground offered a firm tripod to the rifle, and produced far more accurate fire than could be maintained by a soldier standing up, breathing hard, and with the muzzle of his gun wavering around as he picked out a target.

Infantry combat would never be quite the same again. As A.H. Atteridge remarked, writing in 1915:

> After these terrible days the old close order was doomed. The skirmishing line became henceforth recognised as the firing line. Instead of merely clearing the way for lines and masses of troops to follow, it was gradually to work its way forward, fed from the rear by reinforcements to replace its losses. It was to be just dense enough to bring as many rifles as possible into action. It was to be supported by other lines in the same open order from which it could be fed with men and ammunition, and the decision would be produced by its beating down the fire of the opposing enemy, and as this return fire weakened the moment would come when the supports in rear could go forward with the firing line to clear the hostile position.
>
> This new kind of fighting evolved itself at first without any precise orders or directions. Officers and men found they could only get forward by opening out, feeding the firing line, and working onwards from cover to cover. In the battles of earlier days it was only the skirmisher who could lie down behind a rock or bank under fire to take cover; for the officers and men of the main fighting line such an attitude would have been regarded as cowardly. But under the storm of bullets from new rifles, taking cover became a necessity. For the German Army of 1870 battle experiences gave very plain lessons, which however were only learned with much sacrifice of life. In the second stage of the war the Staff began to embody these lessons in provisional regulations and orders.

A good example of the latest practice was by described by Prince Kraft zu Hohenlohe-Ingelfingen, during an attack by two battalions of the *Franz* regiment at Le Bourget in October 1870:

> The officer commanding this regiment had already practised the attack ... Accordingly he sent forward the whole of the leading line, which consisted of two companies, in thick swarms of skirmishers, and made them advance over the open ground in two parts (by wings) which alternately ran in 300 paces. After each rush the whole wing which made it, threw itself down, and found cover among the high potatoes: there they recovered their breath while the other wing

rushed in. As soon as they arrived within range of the needle gun [a rifle whose cartridge was activated by a needle-type striker], the wing which was lying down opened a fire of skirmishers on that edge of the village which they were attacking. I can still remember, as I write, the delight which we felt as from our positions we watched this attack which had been so carefully thought out, and was so well carried through. The best thing was that, as the commander of the regiment assured me, these troops suffered no loss up to the time when they reached the edge of the village.

It was also clear that the balance of power between the various 'arms of service' was altering – indeed, had altered. Whilst at the start of the nineteenth century the cavalry had, often correctly, been identified as a battle-winning weapon, its performance in 1870 had been at best uncertain. Whilst cavalry could certainly get from one point to another more quickly than the infantry, this was essentially a tactical rather than a grand strategic advantage. Any army that wanted to go a long way in the European theatre would now undoubtedly do so by train or ship. Cavalry clearly maintained a significant niche, particularly as scouts and mounted infantry were able to spot the enemy and create flexible outposts and screens that covered other formations very effectively. Nevertheless, the old near-monopoly of the rider as order carrier was under threat. Messages could now be sent from town to town, if not from unit to unit, by Samuel Morse's telegraph. Indeed, the Berlin Treaty of 1851 had long since produced a modified version of 'Morse Code', which (unlike the original American Morse) contained accented letters and other measures, making the transmission of European languages easier.

Yet it was in the actual clash of arms (what had been its old charging 'heavy' or 'battle' cavalry role) that the reputation of mounted troops was most in jeopardy. Horsemen could be stopped by bullets and shells very effectively, and when the men shooting at them were doing so from inaccessible cover, a cavalryman who remained on his steed was powerless to do anything about it except ride away as quickly as possible. The best practice for the most 'modern' cavalry was therefore to get off the horse when it ceased to be useful, and start using rifles – much to the chagrin of the traditionalists.

That the sabre in particular was long past its best was ably demonstrated by the French Colonel T. Bonie. Examination of German medical corps statistics from the Franco-Prussian conflict showed that of 65,000 reported casualties on their lists, only six died and 212 were wounded by swords. This suggested that just one-third of one per cent of the damage on the battlefield was inflicted by the edged weapons of the cavalry, and those that were actually killed in this way were a vanishingly small proportion of the total.

Over the next few years the infantryman's firearm became ever more effective, and by the 1880s most powers had adopted a magazine rifle. Cavalry tended to follow suit with abbreviated versions of the longer infantry rifles. The German army, hitherto armed with a single-shot, 1871 model Mauser, moved on to an improved 1884 type during the later part of the decade. This had an eight-round tube magazine under the barrel. Nevertheless, it was soon surpassed in technical excellence by the French 1886 model Lebel, which used a more-powerful cartridge of smokeless powder. In a spurt of breakneck development, the Germans replied with the swift appearance of the *Gewehr 88*, an 1888 model which married many of the benefits of the recent Mauser and Mannlicher patterns, including the latest 'box' magazine. The last German rifle to be introduced before the outbreak of the First World War was arguably a design classic: the *Gewehr 98* Mauser. This was highly accurate and provided with sights for shooting at anything up to 2,000 metres, though only the best shots could hope to score hits on anything but extremely large targets at such prodigious range. Long and elegant, the *G98* had a five-round box magazine integral to the wooden furniture. From 1905 the *G98* was brought fully up to date to use the latest 'S-Patrone', a cartridge with a pointed, streamlined bullet. Though the emphasis in training was on deliberate, carefully sighted fire, a novice could easily manage five or more aimed rounds in a minute and trained shooters, ten. Fitted with one of the several models of sword or knife bayonet, the rifle was also well calculated to give maximum reach in a bayonet fight.

It was also during the last decade of the nineteenth century and first decade of the twentieth that the machine gun was finally and decisively embraced by the German military. The French *Mitrailleuse* had played a modest part in the Franco-Prussian War, but this was not a true 'machine' gun as it required hand crank-ing like the Gatling of old. It had also been deployed on carriages with large wheels, like a light artillery piece. Truly automatic weap-ons, which continued to fire as long as a trigger was depressed and ammunition was in the feed mechanism, dated from the invention of Hiram S. Maxim's famous gun in the early 1880s. Early examples reached Germany not long afterwards, but, initially at least, lacked a champion to push them forward, or a recognised tactical purpose. Trials at Spandau arsenal in 1888 fascinated observers, but led to no immediate orders.

In 1894, however, Prince Albert Edward, later to be King Edward VII, visited the arsenal in the company of the Kaiser for a further display. This time a Maxim gun was set up in competition with Gatling, Nordenfelt, and Gardner guns. As Maxim himself later explained:

> Three hundred and thirty-three rounds were to be fired from each gun at a target at a range of two hundred metres. The old Gatling gun was worked by four men, and got through with the cartridges in little less than a minute. The same number of men fired the same number of rounds in the Gardner gun in little over a minute. The Nordenfelt was also fired and did just about the same. Then one man advanced, took his seat at the trail of the Maxim gun, touched a button and 333 cartridges went off in less than half a minute. They examined the targets and found that the hand worked guns had made bad targets because the guns themselves had participated in the action of the lever or crank. All the projectiles from the Maxim gun were in the bull's-eye and the whole centre of it had been shot away. The Emperor walked back, examined the gun, and, placing his finger on it, said: 'That is the gun – there is no other.'

With this Imperial endorsement some purchases of Maxim guns were now made, the Navy being one of the first customers. At first the Prussian War Ministry gave land service Maxims to the artil-lery to determine what their 'successful purpose' might be in battle. Probably correctly, the artillery branch failed to identify the weapon as suitable to its arm of service, and passed the new guns on to the *Jäger* (literally 'hunter' – but better translated as 'light infantry') battalions in 1898. Various manoeuvres and tests followed, provoking the initial conclusion that machine guns were best grouped in units of six, so that some guns of the group would keep firing even if one or more suffered mechanical malfunction in action. In 1899 Friedrich von Bernhardi, in his book *Our Cavalry in the Next War*, was one of several voices to speak up in favour of giving some machine weapons to the mounted regiments. For the time being therefore, the home of the machine gun would be with the *Jäger*, cavalry or fortress troops, depending on circumstance.

To some extent the rather uncertain footing of the machine gun in the German military was made more sure with the turn of the century, for by then there were a number of combat examples from other parts of the world which enthusiasts could point to as showing the utility of the new weapon. A 1901 model Maxim was adopted by the army, and, given home production of the gun, development and procurement were significantly eased. By 1904 there were sixteen army machine gun detachments. A new model of machine gun appeared in 1908, and it was this which would bear the main burden of service in World War I. It was now all too apparent that whatever had been achieved in the 1870s with single-shot weapons would, if anything, be far surpassed by the new generation of efficient 'repeating' and 'machine' firearms. Whilst there was continued worry that magazines and swift shooting would lead to profligate expenditure of ammunition, even bloodier battles were a near certainty.

Despite these inventions and realisations, the argument between solid and open battle formations was by no means resolved. Periodically, the subject would be revisited by the critics of dispersion, such as Jakob Meckel and Fritz Honig, with the result that the drill regulations of 1888 were no unequivocal endorsement of the skirmish line as a battle-winning technique. In 1900, following British defeats at the hands of Boer irregulars, the whole matter would be reopened again. Indeed so far did interest in 'Boer tactics' extend that in 1902 General von Moltke mounted an exercise at Doberitz outside Berlin to test similar methods. Later the 'Boer attack' was demonstrated at Tempelhof to the Kaiser, who, being a great enthusiast of many a novelty, endorsed the idea immediately. Nevertheless, it is arguable that in their German incarnation 'Boer tactics' were very much a watered-down version of what had happened on the veldt – they involved many more men in a far smaller space, used relatively little of what might now be called 'field craft', and were practised in the abstract rather than learned practically. Moreover, critics now raised the argument that firepower was being misunderstood. As one contributor to the *Military Weekly* put it: 'Isn't firepower cover of a sort ?' Even the cavalry arm now enjoyed something of a resurgence.

Before long, there were new, foreign models to consider. In the Russo-Japanese War of 1904 to 1905 the Japanese triumphed, apparently using techniques which were not dissimilar to those in use by the German Army. The great siege at Port Arthur helped stimulate interest in mortars, grenades, heavy artillery and other equipment. It also led to a rapid expansion in the number of machine guns – up to an establishment of six per regiment with the line infantry, and six per battalion in the *Jäger*. However, the battles in Manchuria did not appear to invalidate existing infantry tactics. Certainly, siege warfare had played its part, but masterful infantry action had carried the day when it seemed to matter. The war had been costly, but this appeared only to vindicate the idea that tactics needed modification, rather than a total revision.

The upshot of experience, both German and international, was that the *Drill Regulations* of 1906 were something of a hybrid between solid lines and true dispersion. As the company instructions explained:

The change from close to extended order is effected through the formation of skirmish lines. In these the intervals between skirmishers may differ. If the interval be not designated in the command, two paces are taken; if any other interval is desired it must be ordered. Loose skirmish lines result if the interval is greater than two paces, and compact ones if less. Very large intervals increase the difficulty of leading; the minimum interval must still permit the skirmisher free use of his piece ... In extended order the soldier is not bound rigorously to a definite place, nor to a strict military carriage, nor is the handling of the piece to be strictly in accordance with the prescribed manual. On the contrary, he is required to be dextrous in the use of his weapon and in utilising the terrain, self reliant, and unremitting in attention to his leaders and observation of the enemy. Judgement, self reliance, and boldness must be awakened in the breast of the young soldier and in the course of his service be continually strengthened.

Such deployments would put particular emphasis on the role of the junior leader, their positions in the firing line being whatever was rendered necessary by the enemy's fire, with all 'Gefreiter [lance corporals] and especially suitable men [being] trained as squad leaders'. When an individual took up a firing position the key consideration was that he obtain 'effective fire', subordinating 'all considerations of cover' to this end. Only when not firing were soldiers to take up optimum positions for both screening themselves from view and enemy fire. In open country it was assumed that when under fire soldiers would go prone, and that they would be trained in the use of the entrenching tool, so as to provide cover rapidly 'even when lying down'.

Fire training for the individual marksman was deemed of great significance, and to this end it was recommended: 'the rifle must be placed in the hands of the recruit a few days after his arrival'. Primary training involved the 'fundamental principles' of small-arms fire, use of ground, target recognition and distance estimation. Once some facility had been obtained in loading and aiming, troops were to be practised on various types of ground, with simple attack and defence battle manoeuvres included. No time was to be wasted: 'the soldier must be trained to load quickly, to adjust the sight rapidly and accurately, and to aim promptly and calmly against targets which are able to open fire quickly'. How rapid the actual firing was to be was largely dictated by the conditions. Long range, poor light and long periods of action required greater care with aim-taking and economy of ammunition expenditure. Movement of the enemy would, however, be likely to provide opportunities where 'increased rapidity of fire' was well rewarded by its effect. The fastest shooting was needed in the attack during final preparation for a charge; in the defence, to check the enemy during any sudden close encounter and during a pursuit. Commanders were expected to observe the fall of shot and reaction of the opposition by means of field glasses, and correct the men accordingly.

When platoons were in extended order it was likely that different conditions would apply to different parts of the front, some squads being completely under cover, others able to observe the enemy. This would frequently make 'uniform movement' impossible, and fire control difficult. Under such circumstances each squad leader was expected to control the fire of his squad, and 'to utilise without command, every opportunity which presents itself for approaching the enemy, and to support each movement of the neighbouring squads by means of his fire'. Volleys were seldom practical on the battlefield, but might be useful where the enemy was to be taken by surprise.

Organised fire and movement was certainly part of the overall plan, but usually by platoons whenever possible. As paragraph 170 of the *Drill Regulations* explained:

> After the platoon has opened fire, well prepared platoon rushes, supported by the fire of neighbouring units, form the simplest and quickest means of advancing. When platoon rushes become difficult, subdivision of the front into smaller units advancing alternately will become necessary. The manner in which the half platoons or squads then advance will be irregular and varied. They can, while rushing forward, spread out as much as the fire of neighbouring detachments permits and unite again under cover. They can advance by file, or even individually, and also gain ground by creeping.

When commanded to make a rush, troops were expected to close the bolts of their rifles and shut their cartridge boxes without specific orders, moving on the command 'forward march, march'. Hereupon, 'the skirmishers jump up and rush forward'. The length of each rush was to be as long as possible under the specific circumstances, but this was seldom more than eighty metres. Very short rushes were useful in that they permitted the men to go prone again very quickly, affording the enemy little time to aim and fire at them.

Getting as near as possible to pour in fire was seen as the surest way to 'demoralise' the enemy, but an actual charge and close to contact was seen as the usual conclusion to a successful action. Charges by complete units were commonly ordered by the company commander, and could be delivered in close order. They would begin with the fixing of bayonets, and a rapid advance at about 120 paces per minute. Drums and bugles would sound the signal for 'advance quickly'. When the assaulting troops reached the best distance from the enemy the command 'Charge ... Bayonet! Hurra!' was to be given. At this,

> the leading rank charges bayonet [levels weapons at the enemy], everyone continually huzzaing, rushes on the enemy for the hand to hand encounter, until the command 'Company Halt' is given. The two front ranks bring their pieces to the 'ready'. If the enemy is beaten, a pursuing fire is, by command, opened as soon as possible, and if space is available the troops are deployed.

Perhaps surprisingly, 'cold steel' was by no means dead as a tactical concept in the run-up to war. In 1911 the respected tactician Colonel Balck even went so far as to state:

> The soldier should not be taught to shrink from the bayonet attack, but to seek it. If the infantry is deprived of the *arme blanche*, if the impossibility of bayonet fighting is preached, and the soldier is never given an opportunity in time of peace of defending himself, man to man, with his weapon in bayonet fencing, an infantry will be developed, which is unsuitable for attack and which, moreover, lacks a most essential quality, viz., the moral power to reach the enemy's position.

Part of the argument was that the bayonet was the ultimate boost to confidence. It might be true that few men would be killed, or even injured, by a bayonet charge – but if the enemy turned and fled the job was done. Close action also seemed to support the idea of close formations, and the advantage of mass. As late as 1912 there were still influential voices speaking up for greater, rather than reduced, numbers of troops in a given space on the battlefield. The Chief of the Bavarian General Staff, Konrad Krafft von Dellmensingen, was certainly not alone when he suggested that the existing infantry tactics were not sufficiently aggressive and that with dispersal 'everything flits and falls apart in endless space'.

According to Atteridge, reviewing the struggle of 1914 very soon after the event, it was the question of density that proved critical:

The German drill books and army regulations never explicitly adopted the return to close order for which Meckel pleaded. But at the German manoeuvres for years before the war, it was quite evident that the theory had considerable influence on the accepted methods of battle leading. Dense firing lines supported at short range by troops in close order were a feature of these manoeuvre battles.

To put the matter very simply, the accepted theory seems to be this. There is, say, a thousand yards of front available. If a firing line is formed such as we used in South Africa, there might be two hundred rifles in action on this frontage. It would be easy for each man to find cover and they would thus form a dispersed target for hostile fire. But on the same frontage one might put four times the number of men in the line – not necessarily the evenly dressed line of the drill ground, of course – and though more men would thus be exposed to fire, the volume of fire would be four times the heavier. The German argued that the denser firing line would crush out the fire of its dispersed opponent and inflict loss not only on the men in action, but on the supports reinforcing them. We have seen the result of this theory of the fire-fight in the battles of the present war, where the Germans have almost invariably pushed forward closely arrayed firing lines, which gave our men the impression that they were 'coming on in crowds'.

Though the latest theory prescribed a distance between men skirmish firing, the numbers of men deployed led to overcrowding, and old custom died hard. Though clearly encouraging what amounted to a form of fire and movement, and 'skirmish' lines, the 1906 regulations did indeed assume that, 'one can scarcely be too strong for the attack'. Commanders were therefore recommended that a company, while attacking, would occupy no more than a frontage of 150 metres 'at most', whilst an entire brigade of six battalions could be pushed home through a space of 1,500 metres. Such cramped deployment could easily make a nonsense of contradictory, and arguably more 'modern' instructions, to allow men and squads to act with initiative and secure their own cover. A number of memoirs and letters described how some units of German infantry early in the war were actually ordered to advance 'cloth touching', that is, with the uniform of one man's arm in contact with the next. Predictably, there was now no space where poorly aimed bullets could whizz between the files. As one British infantryman in Belgium would later explain: 'You'd see a lot of them coming in a mass on the other side of the canal and you just let them have it'.

One of many on the receiving end the 'other side of the canal' was Captain Walter Bloem of the 12th Grenadiers. By advancing out of woods, and then going prone, he managed to work his men to within about 500 yards of the enemy, though not without cost. Then he gave the order 'Advance by short rushes from the right'. He testified:

> From now on the English fire gradually weakened, almost ceased. No hail of bullets greeted each rush forward, and we were able to get within 150 yards of the canal bank. I said to Graser: 'Now we'll do one more thirty yard rush, all together, then fix bayonets and charge the houses and the canal banks'. The enemy must have been waiting for this moment to get us all together at close range, for immediately the line rose it was as if the hounds of hell had been loosed at us, yelling, barking, hammering as a mass of lead swept in amongst us. 'Down!' I shouted and on my left I heard through the din Graser's voice repeating it. Voluntarily and in many cases involuntarily, we all collapsed flat on the grass as if swept by a scythe.
>
> Previously after each rush Graser had brightened us up with a commentary of curses and cheery chatter, but now there was a noticeable silence on my left. 'Graser!' I called out. No answer. 'Where is *Leutnant* Graser?' And then from among the cries and groans all around came a low voiced reply: '*Leutnant* Graser is dead, sir, just this moment. Shot through the head and heart as he fell'. … From now on matters went from bad to worse. Wherever I looked, right or left, were dead or wounded, quivering in convulsions, groaning terribly, blood oozing from fresh wounds.

This was no isolated experience. Surveying the carnage at Longwy Wurttemberger, Ernst Nopper was moved to remark:

> We are walking over much of the battlefield and we can see what a
> colossal number of victims this battle has cost us. There are whole
> rows of our fellows lying there, especially in the village which is
> totally burned out. ... I don't want to record these shameful horrors
> here but I have not seen anything as sad as this battlefield with so
> many victims who are dead and wounded and in spite of our victory
> this makes us all feel dejected.

Total German casualties for the period August to November 1914
would be well in excess of half a million; of these about a hundred
thousand were dead. Some individual regiments came closer to
annihilation than decimation: the 16th Bavarian suffered almost
3,000 casualties – about seventy per cent of its total strength during the late autumn of 1914. Losses like this, and the halting of the
offensive on the Marne, would be what *Oberst* Max Bauer would
look back on as the '*Marnes Katastrophe*'. To put these enormous, and
hitherto unprecedented, figures in perspective these four months
had far exceeded the German fatalities of the entire Franco-Prussian
War in which 43,000 are thought to have died on the battlefield, and
28,000 of their wounds later. The contrasts in terms of relative success were greater still – the war of 1870 had brought the Prussians
to the gates of Paris, and later the total capitulation of France. The
campaign of 1914 led essentially to the capture of most of Belgium,
and to the engagement of Britain and Russia as well as France.

Casualties in thousands are always difficult to apprehend in
human terms, and detailed and reliable figures for First World War
German losses are notoriously difficult to obtain. As a side light on
tactics such broad-brush material is also of dubious utility. In the
microcosm losses become both more human and more meaningful
as a barometer of what campaigns and weapons were inflicting on
the human form. One of the best documented small-scale surviving
examples must be the *Verlustliste*, or casualty list, of the first company of the Brunswick *Infanterie-Regiment Nr 92*, during the march
through France and Belgium. The list was originally compiled by
Unteroffizier Walter Voigt, an NCO of the company. This covers the
period of just under three weeks from 22 August to 11 September
1914, and is statistically convenient for the researcher as precisely
100 losses are enumerated. Of these, twenty, or exactly one-fifth,

were *krank*, signifying sickness in all its various forms. Though there were cases of stomach complaints and fevers it appears that the biggest single group were various types of foot ailment, occasioned no doubt by lengthy marches. Seven 'losses' were men who had gone missing, though at least two of these managed to return to the unit within a couple of days. There were sixty-three wounded and ten dead. Interestingly, Voigt, ever the conscientious list maker, detailed wherever possible what had caused whom to be wounded or killed, and where the victim had been struck. So it was that we know that of the battle casualties at least thirty were hit by bullets, and at least twenty-two by shells or shrapnel. As one might expect, shots through the chest and abdomen were a common cause of fatality, eight of the dead being killed in this way, a ninth by a shell splinter to the head. One unique casualty was *Unteroffizier* Stotmeister, the only man in the unit to be bayoneted: a stab through the right calf from which he recovered. NCOs and senior privates appear to have been slightly over represented amongst the casualties, twenty-one of them being put *hors de combat*. Officers were even more likely to be hit. *Leutnant* von Kotze was killed, whilst *Hauptmann* von Hanstein and trainee officer Welge were both wounded by shells.

In total, something approaching forty per cent of the entire company manpower was lost, although the relatively few actually killed and the nature of some of the wounds suggests that perhaps half or more of the casualties would have been fit for military service at some later date. *Reservist* Wahlert; *Unteroffizier* Schulze; *Unteroffizier* Wille; *Reservist* Zimnol; *Gefreiter* Koschinsky and a couple more 'other ranks' all had treatment to minor wounds, mainly shrapnel or bullet grazes, to legs, arms and shoulders, but remained '*bei der Truppe* '(at their posts with the company). It may also be speculated that *Musketier* Rossmann's 'stomach catarrh', and most of the foot damage, was of a temporary nature. Whether Reservist Schunemann was able to handle a gun again with a damaged trigger finger remains unknown.

With the failure of all-out aggression, strategic bankruptcy beckoned; but to be fair to the German High Command, Schlieffen, and especially the hapless von Moltke, who was quietly dropped on health grounds in September 1914, the problem of troop density and manoeuvre space was well nigh insoluble given the conditions obtaining at the outbreak of war. Technology had given the infantry, and even more particularly the artillery, longer range and quicker firing weapons than ever before. At the same time, armies were bigger than ever. On the Western Front each side could comfortably put a million men into the field straight away – or to express this in another manner, about 2,500 men for each mile of the line. More than a man for every yard, and in his hands a quick-firing weapon with a range of hundreds of yards. Every inch of the front could thus be swept by rifle bullets, to which had to be added machine guns and shell fire. More recruits and reserves followed, more than doubling the forces and increasing the strategic log jam. It was also the case that in 1914 the overall strengths on the Western Front were in deadly equilibrium; the combined armies of France and Britain, plus the remnant of the Belgian, being able to balance out the numbers of men that Germany was able to commit given the existence of an Eastern Front.

Railways did provide quick movement behind the front, but they also channelled huge numbers down narrow geographic lanes, and from rail head to battlefield front line the marching columns moved at walking pace, as – or more – vulnerable than ever. There was little option for manoeuvre, and rarely anything that could genuinely be called a flank. Moreover, balloons, aircraft, field glasses and spies could now detect movement more easily, whilst telegraph and telephones passed on this knowledge far more quickly than any army could march. Solid fronts and lack of real surprise were in retrospect not unexpected results.

In most places, digging in and the commencement of static warfare was at first a pre-programmed, even spontaneous, reaction by individual units under fire. It was a simple choice between staying on the surface and dying quickly, or making the best of any cover that could be used or dug, and hoping to survive in the longer term. Soon, however, this was accepted as official policy at the highest level. As the new Chief of the General Staff Erich von Falkenhayn explained:

GHQ was fully conscious of the disadvantages involved by the transition to trench war. It was chosen purely and simply as the lesser evil ... the transition to trench warfare was not effected by the independent decision of the Chief of the General Staff, but under the stern pressure of necessity.

Given this circumstance, his eventual objective would be to turn the situation to Germany's advantage, using interior lines of communication to build up strength on one front or another, and by economising in other areas held by trench lines, then deliver 'hard, well-prepared blows' against 'sections of the enemy'. This certainly had an appeal, particularly where the overall balance of numbers was equal, and indeed began to move in favour of the Entente, the gross populations of which significantly outnumbered those of the Central Powers. Nevertheless, attempting to obtain local superiority of numbers on a sector would lead to masses of men in small areas, and what might now be called an extremely 'target-rich' environment. Without a new tactical approach it would be as likely to exacerbate the problem as to offer a solution.

The key document for German troops tasked to dig in was the standard manual *Feld-Pioneerdienst Aller Waffen* ('Field Pioneer Work for All Arms') published in Berlin in December 1911. Numerous photographs and accounts of France and Flanders in 1914 and 1915 attest how much this book was still taken as a model, and indeed how much that was apparently new in the autumn of the first year of war was actually tried and tested practice. According to *Feld-Pioneerdienst*, one of the key purposes of field works was to allow troops to hold with 'relatively little effort' ground which had been taken. Attackers attempting to evict troops who had constructed such positions would thus expend far greater energy and blood than those they sought to remove. This fitted exactly the strategy which had been forced, albeit unwillingly and unintentionally, upon the German command.

The 'primary requirement' in positioning field works was a 'free and open field of fire'. Naturally, the best field of fire to be obtained was found by digging the *Schutzengraben* (fire trenches) near the crest of a rise. *Verbindungsgraben* ('connecting' or 'communication' trenches) would provide covered access to the rear, and natural cover such as rises and foliage could be made use of to disguise the actual positions of the works. In the ideal plan the front line *Schutzengraben* were given *Schulterwehren* (traverses) at eight- to ten-metre intervals, half a metre thick. These acted as protection against enfilading fire, and the explosion of shells and grenades, the effects of which would thereby be limited to relatively short sections of the line. How deep the fire trenches might be depended on topography, and how long the troops had to prepare them. Where the water table was high and time limited, the actual depth excavated below the surface might be as little as thirty centimetres with a protective bank or breastwork built up to the fore. If possible, however, the trenches were excavated to a full 180 centimetres, enough to completely cover most men walking erect, and fire steps were created to allow the occupants to shoot over, or through, the parapet. In German usage the steps or *Stufe* could double as impromptu seating; they were supposed to be forty centimetres wide, and were sometimes therefore known as *Sitzstufe*, or 'sitting steps'.

In the textbook, fully developed trench system, the front line *Schutzengraben* were linked by a communication trench to a cover trench or *Deckungsgraben* in the rear. Short spurs off the main communication trenches led to various special posts. These included the *Abort*, or latrine; communication posts with telephones, or *Fernsprechstelle*; and a *Verbandraum*, or dressing station. As in the equivalent British synthesis, also published in 1911, the rationale of the field works was not negative or passive. On the contrary: trenches were seen as ideal fire positions allowing the troops best use of their weapons, and potentially as jumping-off points, particularly where successive positions could be dug forward with the ultimate purpose of overrunning an enemy fort or defensive work.

Years of literature, memoirs of the most excruciating suffering, and the retrospective retributions of politicians and generals, have led us to the rather simplistic conclusion that trench warfare was the key evil of the Great War. 'Trench' indeed has tended to become a lazy shorthand for pointless warfare. Yet it may be reasonably and convincingly argued that trench warfare itself was not the problem. The solid lines of trenches were more a symptom of the strategic and tactical problem. Neither side had known what to do when mobile warfare came to an unexpected halt; it was only logical that they should dig in, thereby minimising their losses, and holding, in the most effective way they knew how, the ground they already had. How this stasis could be overcome became the main military issue for the next three years.

2

Confronting Stasis

With the digging of the trench lines of the Western Front, the war came to a standstill, but only in the geographic sense. For almost as soon as the first trenches were dug it was apparent that the old tactics of fighting fire with fire were weak, or at worst completely inappropriate. Attacks against solid trench lines, or even against lines of troops in hastily scraped cover stood little chance of success. Statistical probability seemed to have come down ineluctably on the side of the defence. As one German officer put it in a letter home in October 1914:

> The brisk, merry war to which we have all looked forward for years has taken an unforeseen turn. Troops are murdered by machines, horses have almost become superfluous. … The most important people are the pioneers … the theories of decades are shown to be worthless, everything is done differently now.

Alarmingly, French calculations of January 1915 suggested that if troops armed with modern magazine rifles, defending a properly constructed fire trench, were assaulted by a body twelve times their number across open ground, the defenders would almost certainly be triumphant. For if the soldiers in the trench were able to open a steady fire at 800 metres, they would hit a number of the enemy roughly equal to themselves before the latter had succeeded in coming on two hundred metres. A similar mass would be felled as the enemy traversed the next 200 metres. The attacking troops, still several hundred metres away from the trench line, would be unable to score more than a trivial number of hits upon the trench garrison, the need to move forward and the cover provided by the trench making the target exceedingly small and difficult.

Paradoxically, the many wounded were more likely to be an impediment to the attackers than the relatively few who fell stone dead. Quick fatalities made little noise and demanded little immediate attention, medical or otherwise, from their comrades. Badly wounded men needed help, got in the way of the advance, and made a horribly demoralising scene. As infantryman August Hopp recorded: 'One gets by degrees so callous about death that one hardly looks round when anybody falls. The thing one minds most is the lamentations of the badly wounded when one can't do anything for them'. Statistics from various combatant powers during 1915 suggest that rather less than a quarter of battle casualties died instantly or rapidly, almost three-quarters being various categories of wounded. Perhaps one in twenty of all casualties 'died of wounds' hours or weeks after the event, with a similar number becoming, in one way or another, 'missing'.

Once the assaulting ranks had closed to within about 400 metres of a trench their problems mounted, for now the defending troops were presented with a bigger target, and little correction for range would be required. The defenders could expect to take down another portion of the enemy, equal to their own strength, as the enemy closed to 300 metres. In the twenty seconds it took the attackers to come forward, each defender could expect to loose off three or four shots, and the chances were that one of these would hit home, given the bulk of the target. For each additional hundred metres the attacker succeeded in advancing, the casualties would multiply, until the murderous last hundred.

Here, provided they maintained their nerve, even very poor shots would hit something, and rounds would be ever more likely to penetrate through more than one rank of the attackers. Bullets aimed short might plough on or ricochet upwards. Hesitant attackers provided sitting targets, whilst those dashing onward would be quite unable to fire back.

There was every likelihood that troops out in the open taking such horrendous losses would turn and flee, or drop and hug the ground. Meanwhile, the trench defenders, protected by their walls of earth and watched by their officers, would be unlikely to break. Indeed, they might well feel that they were far safer where they were, rather than clambering back up out of their positions. By the time the bravest of the brave reached a trench line they were likely to be reduced to a number similar to, or fewer than, their adversaries. Having advanced a considerable distance, many of their own officers and NCOs would have become casualties, which would have inevitably created disorganisation as well as adding to the physical and psychological exhaustion of those who remained. Unless they were exceptionally well-informed, they would be at a disadvantage upon entering the defender's labyrinth, where the trench garrison knew every twist and turn, and had stockpiles of ammunition and other supplies on hand for just such an eventuality. Where the rifles of the trench defenders were supplemented by machine guns it was extremely unlikely that any attackers advancing using conventional tactics, would get within a hundred metres of a trench, even if they had outnumbered the defenders by a ratio of fourteen to one at the outset.

The failings of trench warfare affected all of the armies, though to a varying extent. For the Russian soldiers facing the German defenders in the East, the crushing attacks mounted in the old style proved absolutely catastrophic. Karl von Wiegand, a reporter for the United Press at the battle of Wirballen in Russian Poland in October 1914 was a witness:

> For the first time I sensed the intoxication of battle. ... On came the Slav swarm – into the range of the German trenches, with wild yells and never a waver. Russian battle flags – the first I had seen – appeared in the front of the charging ranks. The advance line thinned and the second line moved up. Nearer and nearer they swept towards the German positions. And then came a new sight! A few seconds later came a new sound. First I saw a sudden, almost grotesque, melting of the advancing lines. It was different to anything that had taken place before. The men literally went down like dominoes in a row. Those who kept their feet were hurled back as though by a terrible gust of wind. Almost in the second that I pondered, puzzled, the staccato rattle of machine guns reached us. My ear answered the query of my eye.
>
> For the first time the advancing lines hesitated, apparently bewildered. Mounted officers dashed along the line urging the men forward. Horses fell with the men. I saw a dozen riderless horses

dashing madly through the lines, adding a new terror. Another horse was obviously running away with his officer rider. The crucial period for the section of the charge on which I had riveted my attention probably lasted less than a minute. To my throbbing brain it seemed an hour. Then, with the withering fire raking them, even as they faltered, the lines broke. Panic ensued. It was every man for himself. The entire Russian charge turned and went tearing back to cover and the shelter of the Russian trenches. I swept the entire line of the Russian advance with my glasses – as far as it was visible from our position. The whole advance of the enemy was in retreat, making for its entrenched position. After the assault had failed and the battle resumed its normal trend, I swept the field with my glasses. The dead were everywhere. They were not piled up, but were strewn over acres. More horrible than the sight of the dead, though were other pictures brought up by the glasses. Squirming, tossing, writhing figures everywhere! The wounded ...

Official British observation tended to confirm French theory, and what was a well-nigh universal experience. Even before 1914 was out, the instructional publication *Notes from the Front* carried an item explaining, with the aid of an account given by a prisoner, how German attacks were often delivered – and often miscarried. Commonly, the attacking formation came on in three waves, each one being composed of two individual lines of troops, the whole being backed by machine guns. The first wave moved forward quickly, taking most of the punishment meted out by the defence, and exchanging fire. The last wave carried with it shovels and small picks, as well as machine guns. By taking advantage of the progress of those in front, the rear echelon hoped to get as close as possible to the defenders until they too were halted by fire. When stopped they would dig in at once. However, where the ground was open, the distance at which they were halted could well prove to be 800 yards or more from riflemen in cover.

Sometimes an assault would falter even before the troops could see who was firing at them. It was what one soldier called 'running the gauntlet' – not marching, but advancing 'by leaps and bounds'. Twenty-three-year-old student-turned-soldier Alfred Buchalski recounted the attack near Dixmuide, in Belgium in October 1914:

How shall I ever properly describe to you the experiences of the last few days? I should like to give you a complete picture of the whole battle, but only little isolated incidents thrust themselves into the foreground. It was ghastly! Not the actual shedding of blood, nor that it was shed in vain, nor that in the darkness our own comrades were firing at us – no, but the whole way in which a battle is fought is so revolting. To want to fight and not even to be able to defend oneself! The attack, which I thought was going to be so magnificent, meant nothing but being forced to get forward from one bit of cover to another in the face of a hail of bullets, and not to see who was firing them!

The unnerving experience of fighting an unseen enemy was also encountered by Fritz Meese during the same attack:

We have been repulsed, nobody knows how. In front of us is a farm and on the right a road, as far as which we have advanced as gaily confident of victory as if on a parade ground. Forward we went, step by step, upright too, too proud to duck before the continuous whistle of bullets. Then suddenly we were lying in the front line with our machine gun. Our Corporal was killed beside me. On my right 'J' was shot in the arm and I got a bullet through my mess tin. So we lay behind a hedge; were supposed to fire, but could see no enemy. Then came the order: 'Up, march, march to the farm!' There a metallic song was whistling and singing amongst the branches, the house was burning, and behind what was left of the wall were the *Jägers* and the 201st, while machine gun fire was crumbling the wall stone by stone. I tied up first 'N' and then 'R' with the field service dressing … we went farther on, getting into complete disorder, no officers left and comrades falling in rows.

So much that was terrible happened so quickly, that for those in a failing infantry attack, time would often seem to expand and consciousness become heightened. Philosophy student-turned-soldier Kurt Peterson, was well placed to comment:

What experience one goes through during such an attack! It makes one years older! Death roars around one; a hail of machine gun bullets; every moment one expects to be hit; one is certain of it. One's memory is in perfect working order; one sees and feels quite clearly. One thinks of one's parents. Then there rise in every man thoughts of defiance and of rage and finally a cry for help: away with war! Away with this vile abortion brought forth by human wickedness! Human beings are slaughtering thousands of other human beings whom they neither know, nor hate, nor love ...

Not seeing the enemy almost always entailed not knowing exactly where he was. Tactical errors therefore compounded the inability to shoot back with any certainty. Again in Flanders, infantryman Ulrich Timm recalled an attack which was a 'complete failure'. Having 'swarmed out of our trench', with fixed bayonets and shouts of 'Hurrah!', his unit found themselves behind another German formation. Any firing his comrades did therefore impacted more upon the men in front than the enemy. To make matters worse they soon discovered that they were 'a mile or more away from the enemy position when we began storming, so that we were tired before the attack really started'.

It was realised almost immediately that dense formations were a large part of the problem. Empirical observation showed that units that attacked in more open formations, or that spread out under artillery fire, suffered far fewer casualties than those that remained in columns. Within days, middle-ranking commanders were taking unilateral decisions on what posture to adopt, and very quickly these common-sense measures were reflected in official policy. A good example was the orders issued by the Duke of Wurttemberg to Fourth Army on 21 August 1914 warning against poor reconnaissance, premature assault and 'too dense formations'.

One obvious way to reduce the odds that were so stacked in the defenders' favour was the night attack. Most obviously, the cloak of darkness would provide cover against being seen, and what could not be seen could not be accurately engaged. Yet night also offered other advantages, for there was a chance that defenders could be taken by surprise. It was also the case that since attackers seldom had the chance of aimed fire against targets concealed in trenches, they had least to lose by coming on with the bayonet, whilst defenders, if attempting to shoot into the darkness, would inevitably give away their location by the muzzle flash from their weapons.

Night attacks were attempted early in hostilities, with *Lieutnant* Erwin Rommel of the 124th (Wurttemberg) Regiment describing such an attack against the village of Rembercourt on the night of 9 September, 1914. The order to attack was received with relief rather than trepidation, because it, 'promised a release from the hell of French artillery fire'. So it was that:

> In a pouring rain and in pitch darkness, the battalion got ready for the attack ... bayonets were fixed, rifles unlocked. The password was 'Victory or Death'. ... Our men waited anxiously for H hour. By this time they had been soaked to the skin for hours and frozen with cold. Hours passed. Finally at 0300 we got the attack order. In massed formation the battalion plunged down the slope onto the enemy along the railway, overran him, seized the cuts on the Sommaisne-Rembercourt highway, and stormed Hill 287. Wherever the enemy resisted he was dispatched with the bayonet, the rest of the battalion bypassing the local point of resistance. With all four companies in line the battalion occupied Hill 287. No support had materialised on either flank, so both our flanks were exposed. Units were badly mixed and reorganisation proceeded slowly. Dawn began to break and the rain started to let up. The units were digging furiously to provide protection from the French artillery fire which was expected shortly.

During the hours of daylight other methods of obscuring attacking troops were also the subject of experiment. Smoke or fog were obvious candidates for use as cover, but there were also tests with shields – a possibility that had been considered even before the outbreak of war. In at least one instance the large metal shields issued with the standard MG 08 machine guns were detached and used as cover under which small numbers of men crawled forward toward the enemy positions. There were also experiments, similar to those conducted by the French and British, with shields on small wheels. These never became universal, but small, metal, oblong shields did eventually obtain fairly widespread currency. In the German instance, a 1916 model shield, with a shutter for observation and fire and a rear prop enabling it to be put up on any fairly level surface, was issued quite widely. It was rarely used offensively.

Such efforts mirrored the methods of siege engineers and archers, all the way back to the medieval era, who had used 'sap rollers' and pavises in their attempts to approach fortifications in safety. In the early twentieth century, against riflemen in trenches, they were far less successful. The biggest problem was that modern jacketed rifle bullets possessed much more penetrative power than the arrow. The .303-inch round, for example, was perfectly capable of punching through more than a third of an inch of what the manual described as 'best hard steel plate' at close range. Half an inch of mild steel or wrought iron was no significant obstacle to the military rifle bullet at several hundred yards, where house bricks could also be shot through. It would of course have been possible to make shields sufficiently thick and tough to stop any small arms bullet, but then these expensive shelters would have become massively heavy and all but immobile – sitting targets for artillery. Shields also had the significant disadvantage that if they were large enough to cover one or more men, they were also very difficult to hide in any offensive scenario. They could therefore attract fire to targets which many riflemen defending trenches would otherwise have failed to observe. Before the advent of the tank the shield option proved pretty much a tactical dead end, viable only in the most specific and limited of circumstances – such as the static protection of concealed loopholes for snipers. Shields therefore tended to become a reinforcement of trench lines and tools of specialists, rather than a way to launch a serious attack.

Another relatively simple way to improve the odds for attacking entrenched opposition was to attempt to push forward machine guns. These would then bring down fire on the trench from opportune angles, either clearing a section of the enemy line by their own efforts, or acting as a precursor to a more general attack that they could support as it went forward. As the British publication *Notes From the Front, Part III* of February 1915 explained:

The German machine guns are used in the attack with boldness and cleverness; they are pushed up close to the hostile trenches, and in this manner sometimes prepare the way for the infantry attack. They are often used in conjunction with snipers. Machine guns are used in large numbers against one or both flanks of the portion of the position which it is intended to attack. They usually cross their fire, which makes them difficult to locate from the portion of the trench opposite them. One attack was carried out solely by machine guns. The trench was engaged from a flank by six or seven guns, while other machine guns succeeded in working round and enfilading the position.

The exact range is usually obtained by opening bursts of fire as soon as a suitable fire position has been occupied, after which the Germans satisfy themselves by preventing the defenders, as far as possible, from showing above the parapet, thus enabling their own troops to approach in security. The closer they can approach a trench, the more oblique becomes their fire. The duration and volume of the fire depend on the ground over which the advance of their own infantry has to be made, but they are careful to husband their ammunition, as the ammunition supply is the chief difficulty with these guns. When the advance of their own infantry has passed the machine guns, the Germans try to place the latter in positions whence they can assail the enemy as he retires from his trenches, or, alternatively, in the event of a counter-attack, to open fire in such a way as to allow their own infantry to withdraw.

German machine gun instructions composed just a month or two later saw the same issue from the opposite perspective:

> In infantry engagements, when the opposing forces are some distance apart, an entrenched enemy can be attacked only by rifle fire or enfilade machine gun fire, which is then very effective. This is the explanation of the efforts made by both the attacking and defending troops to capture or hold positions which are suitable for enfilade fire. Where this is not possible rifle grenades have been used successfully.

It was reasonably obvious that what a machine gun could accomplish might be better achieved with artillery, and so began the idea of pushing forward field guns in direct support of attacks on trenches. Like so many concepts of the trench war this was not entirely new – the use of artillery over open sights in direct support of infantry had been a staple of battle for centuries. Yet bringing guns closer ran contrary to recent developments: firing from longer ranges (using telescopes, telephones, and even maps, to direct artillery fire) seemed to be the way of the future. Moreover, bombardment from a distance had had the useful effect of making the maximum capital of the superior range of artillery over the range of the rifle. In long-range action, few, if any, of the artillerymen fell victim to small arms, whilst the infantry could be pounded at leisure by the gunners.

Moving artillery up to point-blank range was therefore counter-intuitive in many ways, and left a number of problems to be solved. Not least of these was the fact that a full-sized 77mm field gun or 105mm howitzer was an immense object, on large wheels which were best suited to bowling at good speed down a road when dragged by a team of horses. Moving such a field gun with its crew across shell-pocked ground whilst under fire was highly problem-atic. Producing a new gun, or modifying an existing piece, in such a way that it became small enough to be manhandled and inconspicu-ous on the battlefield therefore became a high priority. In the event, such store was put by the idea that it would be thought worthwhile to develop a whole new experimental unit dedicated to devising tactics, and the use of such *Sturmkanonen* ('assault artillery'). The result would be the first *Sturmabteilung* ('Storm detachment').

If covering the advance of troops and close-range support from other weapons were indirect methods of helping the infantryman onto the enemy position, then giving the individual soldier new weapons and altering his tactics was the direct method. Again, the most important addition to the arsenal was an old one from the annals of siege warfare, reinvented for the modern age. The grenade, as a weapon of siege and storm, had been used from the late medi-eval era. As applied to the trenches it had considerable advantages over rifle and bayonet, not least of which was that the grenadier need not actually see the target he was attempting to destroy. Bombs could be hurled over traverses and rolled in and out of trenches, as well as lobbed over obstacles and the heads of friendly troops.

In 1914 there were already two types of hand grenade in German service: the *Kugelhandgranate Modell 1913,* or ball hand grenade 1913; and the *Diskushandgranate,* or disc hand grenade. The *Kugelhandgranate* was a spherical bomb in the old anarchist mould with a pull fuse on top. Weighing about 800g with a time delay of seven seconds, and made of cast iron, it was best used from, or into, heavy cover. The *Diskushandgranate* was of a rather more imaginative type, being a small, oyster-like iron shell with detonators arranged around the perimeter.

When properly thrown and impacted, it exploded on arrival. For longer range work there were rifle grenades, types 1913 and 1914, which were equipped with rods and could be shot from the standard rifle.

It was not, however, simply a question of handing out grenades and launching a new type of attack overnight. Bombs were in short supply, and as *Feld-Pionierdienst* 1911 made clear, initially the use of grenades was seen essentially as part of engineer or siege work. However, it had already been accepted that the *Pioniere* could have an assault function separate from construction engineering, and this specialisation had been encouraged by Baron Colmar von der Goltz, former head of the Army Corps of Engineers. It therefore quickly became common practice to attach parties, or even individual pioneers, to the infantry. As early as the autumn of 1914 in the Argonne *Leutnant* Hermann Balck recorded how his platoon of the 10th *Jäger* would be joined by a single grenade-armed pioneer every evening, who would man his post in the front line until dawn. Having fulfilled his vigil against French attack he would then depart back to his own company in the morning. In the forefront of attacks against fortified positions, pioneers would attempt to clear the way for their rifle-armed infantry colleagues using axes, wire cutters, and grenades. Before 1914 was out, Pioneer *Leutnant* Walter Beumelberg was able to observe how a man armed with a bag of grenades was at a significant advantage over conventionally armed troops, who were not able to fire at him in a winding trench. Such exploits may well have been inspired by stories of the Russo-Japanese war a decade earlier, which had also had their impact on influencing the commissariat to begin supplying German forces with mortars several years before the onset of European hostilities.

There were too few pioneers and not enough grenades. A short-term answer was for improvised grenades to be manufactured at or near the front – tin cans stuffed with explosive and shrapnel, or wooden handles to which were wired charges. Most were lit by means of a fuse, but fuses needed a means of ignition. Pending the introduction of any more certain method, the homespun grenadiers lit their missiles with a pipe or cigar, which could be kept burning in the mouth during combat. By 1915 the front-made bombs were also being supplemented by emergency home-production models, lit by means of spring igniters and integral red phosphorus matches which could be rubbed on a rough surface to set them afire.

Specifically to get the grenadier onto, or preferably into, the enemy position required exploiting the weapon by means of new tactics, for if grenadiers simply advanced in skirmish lines upon trenches, most of them would suffer the same fate as the riflemen they supplemented or replaced. In 'limited enterprises' the best method was to send grenadiers across to the enemy position under cover of darkness. 'Trench raids' certainly began in 1914, and by 1915 were assuming something of an art form. One such was recorded, by *Landwehr Leutnant* Rust of Infantry Regiment 60, in January 1915:

> We noticed that the enemy trenches were more densely occupied than usual. We had to find out if there was a particular reason for this; if, for example, a French attack had to be anticipated. Volunteers Forward! Koch was first and he was joined by his friend *Unteroffizier* Wozniakowski and *Musketier* Selden from the 5th Company. Rifles were left behind, daggers were carried in boot tops and a number of hand grenades were carried. Crawling along the line of the railway embankment, past the French sentry, they reached the densely occupied trench. Go! It was the work of a moment to throw hand grenades into the middle of the Frenchmen, where they exploded, sending splinters flying in all directions. Loud shouts, confusion and frenzied shooting was the surprised response of the French troops. The sentry, up on the embankment, took fright and blazed away aimlessly into the darkness. The company, which was occupying an advanced strong point could clearly hear the exploding grenades, the shouting and the shooting and began to fear for our brave lads, but they all returned safely.

Where grenade action formed part of a set-piece assault, getting numbers of men across 'No Man's Land' was far more problematic. What was clear, however, was that grenadiers stood a far better chance of survival if they travelled in scattered groups – far less conspicuous, and much easier to conceal in shell holes or other cover as they scurried forward. Ideally, attacking bombers did not show themselves at all, but advanced through depressions in the ground or disused communication trenches from former actions. What had yet to be mastered was the integration of these primitive assault tactics with other new weapons, and a distillation of what had been learned into new tactical theory.

3

Grenades, Flame and Gas: Tactics and Technology

The increasing role of the grenade and its importance *vis-à-vis* fire-arms in trench warfare was recognised and built upon in official German literature during 1915. The battles in the Champagne, for example, produced 2nd German Army's tactical synthesis *Experiences Gained From the September Offensives on the Fronts of the Sixth and Third Armies*, in which we find the following observation regarding the necessity of universal grenade training:

> In beating off an attack, as well as in the capture of lost trenches, hand grenades have always played a most prominent and success-ful part. Men who are not familiar with the use of hand grenades proved more dangerous to themselves and their comrades than to the enemy. They threw their grenades away at random from sheer fright of the unfamiliar weapon. All infantrymen and pioneers must be trained in bombing just as thoroughly as they are with the rifle. An effort should be made to see that every individual man throws at least one live grenade during the course of training. During the defence there was too great a tendency on the part of the men to throw their grenades too soon. First of all rifles must be used, and not until the enemy has approached quite close will hand grenades be employed: it is then that their effect is good.

Typical instructions issued to 3rd Battalion of the 235th Reserve Infantry Regiment in December 1915, show that *Stoss* or 'shock' tactics using grenades were well developed for defence, as well as offence, by this time:

Should the enemy have penetrated into a small portion of the trench, and should the troops on the spot not be able to deal with them by means of the bayonet or hand grenades, the bombing party [*Handgranatentrupp*] should, without waiting for orders, immediately attack the enemy with grenades before it becomes necessary to erect a barricade in the trench. On a signal from their commander the men of the bombing party equip themselves with hand grenades and collect around him.

All men of the party carry their rifles slung, bayonets fixed and daggers ready, with the exception of the two leaders, who do not carry rifles. The latter may carry as many grenades as they can conveniently handle and should, if possible, be armed with pistols. The commander, similarly armed, follows the two leading men. If no pistols are available, the commander, who should cover the two leading men, carries his rifle ready loaded in his hands. The remaining three men follow the others one traverse to the rear; they keep within sight of their commander, and carry as many grenades as possible. When possible the grenades are carried in their boxes. The two leading men advance along the trench in a crouching posture, so that the commander can fire over them. The interval between traverses is crossed at a rush.

If the enemy has penetrated into the trench with a large force, and a continuation of his attack is to be expected, as good a barricade as circumstances permit should be erected. The bombing party should at first remain on the defensive behind this barricade or breastwork. Rifles should be unslung ready for use. The commander and the three rear men should take up position behind the nearest traverse and within sight of the two leading men.

Bombing parties belonging to the platoons in support and in reserve should be stationed somewhere in the vicinity of the communication trenches, and should be brought up to a strength of eight men including the commander.

For offensive action the drill was similar, but the *Handgranatentrupp* commenced their choreographed trench-clearing tactics only when the enemy line was reached. Here they would lead the way down the trench, effectively taking the defenders from the flank, rolling up the line rather than attempting any frontal attack. The team would advance or bomb their way forward, depending on the level of resistance encountered.

That this was no mere theory, and that bombing attacks involving fluidity rather than rigid lines formed part of the repertoire of most units by mid 1915, is demonstrated by many first-hand accounts. Perhaps one of the most famous is that of Erwin Rommel, describing an assault in the Argonne in June of that year in which grenade fighting was actively integrated with intelligent use of terrain and initiative:

> The communication trench assigned to us was exposed to strong hostile fire, and I decided to deviate from my orders in displacing to the side for about one hundred metres. We ran for our lives across the open stretch of ground and found shelter down in the hollow; then, through the communication trench, we rushed into the front line with the French standing barrages bursting all around. The storm troops were lying side by side, and across from us the last gun and mortar shells were bursting. 0845, and our assault moved forward over a wide front. French machine guns poured out their fire; the men jumped around craters, over obstacles and into the enemy position. The assault echelon of our company was hit by machine gun fire from the right and a few fell, but the bulk rushed on, disappearing in craters and behind embankments. My platoon followed. Each man had his load, either several spades or else sacks filled with grenades or ammunition. The French machine gun to the right was still hammering away. We passed through its field of fire and climbed over the walls … The position was a mass of rubble. Dead and wounded Frenchmen lay scattered through the tangle of revetments, timbers and uprooted trees. These revetments had cost many a Frenchman his life. To the right and front of us hand grenade fights were in progress, and from rearward positions French machine guns swept the battlefield in all directions and forced us to take cover … We engaged the garrison of 'Central II'. Our own artillery had ceased firing. A few salvos of hand grenades followed by a charge, and we were in to Central II. Part of the garrison ran down the trench, others fled across the open fields, and the rest surrendered. While part of the outfit worked to widen the trench, the bulk of the assault force kept pressing south.

By the beginning of 1916 grenade supply was much improved, if not entirely perfected, and the number of bomb types much reduced. As *Leutnant* Gerster of Reserve Infantry Regiment 119 put it: 'The makeshift hand grenades available on the outbreak of war disappeared gradually. Factory-made types replaced them: the discus grenade, which gradually disappeared too; the ball-shaped grenade, later relieved by the lighter egg grenade, which could be thrown further, and the stick grenade'. The famous stick or *Stielhandgranate* was soon found to be satisfactory, particularly in the assault, where its thin casing produced little fragmentation and the primary effect was a localised blast, well calculated to disable the recipient without sending splinters back to the thrower. Its stick, easily grasped, also gave the user a satisfyingly long throw. Yet it was not without its faults and teething problems. On the first model, introduced in 1915, the pull cord was simply taped down to the handle, which not only made it susceptible to damp but produced considerable safety problems, as Gerster also reported:

> The safety device of the stick grenade was a constant source of concern and anger for the company commanders. Despite all care, again and again, the firing cord was accidentally caught and pulled on exiting dugouts, or when passing along trenches revetted with wooden hurdles. This ignited the grenade without the carrier being aware of the fact, thus putting him in mortal danger. The star screw catch, which was introduced after much experimentation, finally produced a splendid solution to a problem which was far from insignificant to the infantry.

As was revealed by instructions to the 180th Infantry Regiment issued on 28 February, further refinement was made to bombing tactics during the course of 1916. The normal number of the *Handgranatentrupp* was now increased from seven plus the squad leader, to eight plus leader. The eight men were now divided into two subsections of four. The front subsection was the cutting edge of the *Gruppe*, comprising two selected throwers and two carriers in close support. All were to be equipped with six grenades. When necessary, all four men would throw together, creating short showers of bombs. The lead team's ancillary weapons would include pistols and trench daggers. The rear team of four was made up of carriers and spare men: their ideal equipment was rifle and bayonet, six grenades apiece and twenty-five sand bags secured to their bodies by means of haversack straps.

The *Handgranatentrupp* was instructed to advance along trenches well spread out to minimise casualties from enemy grenades. When they met traverses suspected to be held by the opposition, these were to be 'bombed over', then the number two of the group would call out *'Geraumt!'* (cleared) to the leader. The leader could then give the order to continue the advance. In some instances the leader would be provided with small, white marker flags to be placed at intervals along the top of the trench. These would inform other teams that the section of trench had been cleared, and thus prevent friendly troops from attacking each other. If the advance of the *Handgrenatentrupp* was completely halted by determined resistance, a barricade would be erected across the trench to hold the ground already secured. On the command *'Sandsache vor!'* (sandbags forward) the rear members of the squad would set to work on the 'trench block' using their sandbags. The blockade was usually so positioned that it was put up between the two subsections of the group, with the front team concentrating on holding off the enemy until the construction was complete. Machine gun posts or blockhouses required rather different tactics. In this instance one or two members of the team would be detailed to take up sniping positions, firing on the loopholes of the objective. With the enemy thus occupied the rest of the group would attempt to work around the flanks and rear of the enemy, making tactical use of shell holes and topography. Finally, they would rush the objective from unexpected angles, bombing it into submission.

To learn the new tactics required thorough training – both theoretical and practical. Initially, volunteers were sought for specialised training, but as the importance of the bomb was recognised and numbers of volunteers decreased, bombing training became progressively universal. By the middle of the war it seems likely that most troops had received at least rudimentary instruction. The theoretical part was talks on types of bombs, both German and enemy, and their uses and safety. Practical training was done initially with dummy bombs, which were as much like the live examples as possible but painted red. Sometimes, practice stick grenades were not only painted distinctively but had their heads drilled through, so as to demonstrate to the trainees and instructors that they were not filled.

The ideal training area was the *Handgrenatenstand,* laid out specifically for the purpose, and so designed as to mimic actual battlefield conditions. This might include strong points, wire entanglements, loopholes, sap heads and farm buildings. The first exercises were to get the men to throw properly from standing, kneeling and lying positions, and then to combine this with jumping swiftly in and out of the trenches. Throwing and attacking manoeuvres were carried out not just on voice command, but in response to hand and whistle signals. Grenade handling required particular attention, and the troops were taught always to pick up a grenade with the hand that they intended to use when throwing, since passing a bomb from hand to hand with the fuse lit wasted time and invited dangerous fumbles.

The finer points of technique could be tested using practice bombs with a fuse but no main charge. The normal length of time fuse was five and a half seconds: enough timer to initiate the fuse deliberately and without undue panic; give a good, aimed throw to a decent length; and for the bomb to explode soon after arrival. This was usually a perfectly feasible series of operations in trench-to-trench action, but in the hurly-burly of a grenade duel or when the enemy were swarming over the position, fuses were sometimes found to be too long. Sometimes, a grenade would be thrown and be left fizzing on the ground long enough that the enemy could dive down, or kick the bomb away. At other times, missiles would be hurled at a charging enemy, and, failing to explode immediately, be left behind by the opposition, who simply rushed past as they lay on the ground. Occasionally, a particularly stalwart enemy would succeed in picking up a live bomb and throwing it back at his would-be assailants.

As few of the German bombs were 'percussion' models designed to explode on impact, solving the timing issue was problematic. In some battalions, men were actually taught to pull the fuse and then count away a few seconds before throwing. Sometimes, in order to judge the length of each second more accurately, the count was 22,

23, 24 – *zwei und zwanzig, drei und zwanzig, vier und zwanzig* – rather than a simple, and usually far too quick, *ein, zwei, drei*. Correctly judged, the technique could result in explosions dead on cue, or even make it possible to aim bombs directly at an opponent's body in close action. At army level, however, the counting technique was absolutely forbidden for fear that slow or nervous counters be blown to pieces by their own bombs.

As in other armies, the German High Command eventually became convinced that the troops were becoming too reliant upon the grenade, using it in preference to other weapons even when the tactical situation suggested that grenades were unsuitable for the purpose in hand. As Ludendorff later remarked:

> The excessive use of hand grenades came about because these could be usefully and safely employed from behind shelter, whereas a man using a rifle must leave his cover. In the close fighting of some of our own raids, and also in large-scale attacks by the enemy, where the fighting at any moment came to be man to man, hand grenades were readier weapons for unpractised men and easier to use than rifles, the latter also having the disadvantage of getting dirty easily. One could understand that; but infantry must keep able to hold the enemy off and fight from a distance. When it came to hand-to-hand fighting, the superiority of the enemy in men was much too great. The infantry soldier had forgotten his shooting through use of grenades. He had to relearn it.

Probably the most discussed, but least understood, contribution to the tactical debate in 1915 came from a Frenchman. This was Andre Laffargue's *L'Etude sur L'Attaque*, an extremely influential pamphlet based on the author's experience at Neuville St Vaast in May 1915. The most remarkable thing about this document was not so much what it said, but the fact that within a few months it was available to all the major combatant powers. As an illustration of how the tactics of the Great War were developed by a process of learning from the enemy, and combining the best and most practical elements to be found on the battlefield, it is unsurpassed. In terms of timing it was also approximately coincident with two German documents criticising French methods. These were the somewhat cumbersomely titled: *Proposals For Technical Methods to be Adopted in An Attempt to Break Through a Strongly Fortified Position, Based on Knowledge Acquired From the Errors Which Appear to Have Been Committed By the French During the Winter Campaign in Champagne*, of 18 March 1915; and *Experiences Gained in the Winter Battle in the Champagne from the Point of View of the Organisation of the Enemy's Lines of Defence and the Means of Combating an Attempt to Pierce Our Line*, of 13 May 1915. Little wonder, with wordy and rather anonymous competition like this, that it is the more elegant and rounded *L'Etude* that is better remembered by posterity. Nevertheless, like *L'Etude*, both *Proposals*, and *Experiences Gained* were pretty much common currency to French, German and British tacticians. For whilst *L'Etude* was captured by the Germans, and also translated into English as *A Study of the Attack in the Present State of War*; both of the German documents – themselves based on modification of French methods – were captured by the British and appeared in English translation before the end of 1915. Taken together, they demonstrate how fallacious it is to pretend that new methods were developed in isolation, or indeed that any one power had established a commanding tactical lead at this time.

Laffargue has variously been credited as the originator of both 'infiltration' and 'Stormtroop' tactics, but although his paper is extremely interesting, this is a gross exaggeration. Indeed, one is left wondering if such claims can possibly have been made by anyone who has actually read *L'Etude*. It may be far more reasonably stated that what Laffargue was proposing in 1915 actually came to fruition as the 'big pushes' of 1916. The tactics he detailed undoubtedly have far more in common with the conduct of the battles of Verdun and the Somme than they do with St Quentin or the Lys in 1918. For Laffargue the key problem was that the war had become a siege, and that as in a siege the capture of a single trench or a few yards of ground made very little difference in the overall scheme of things. The simple answer that he proposed was that a proper attack should not 'nibble' at a defensive position, but, in the manner of 'an immense and unlimited assault, delivered on all points of the attacking front', swallow the whole of the enemy ground 'in a single gulp'. To do this required 'overwhelming superiority of fire' at all phases.

Artillery preparation would be crucial: destroying barbed wire entanglements, neutralising or destroying trench garrisons, firing counter-battery shoots, blocking reserves and destroying machine guns as part of their programme. 'Aerial torpedoes' would make sure that deep enemy dugouts, not destroyed by the ordinary artillery, were blocked up as their entrances caved in. The enemy would be kept guessing by pauses in the bombardment, and if necessary 'smoked out' with gas and grenades. Sudden 'deluges' of shells would be particularly effective in surprising the opposition; smoke and gas laid down on enemy batteries would force them to stop firing, or work 'under extremely trying conditions'. For the engagement of enemy machine guns not disabled in the main bombardment, the infantry would have just behind their first wave 'light guns', of 37mm for example, 'drawn by their gunners'. Machine guns and automatic rifles would be pushed right to the front of the attack.

In Laffargue's synthesis, the infantry assault would advance in 'lines of attack' – at least three – followed by a completely fresh echelon using cavalry and 'motor cars' for the breakout beyond the enemy position. The first line of attack would itself be composed of two or more waves; the first advancing not with any great dispersal if the enemy trench was close, but 'rushing half a pace apart'. Where the enemy line was further away, the front wave would come on allowing 'five paces' between each man, these troops being picked for their calmness and 'resolution'. Fifty yards behind would come what can only be described as solid blocks of troops, 'shoulder to shoulder', or at most 'one pace apart'. On leaving their own trenches 'each line' was to 'jump out in turn' and then advance, 'marching in step if possible'. The approach could involve short rushes, but 'marching in correct dressing' was essential. At sixty yards from the enemy the order to charge would be given. All along the line bayonets would be levelled at the enemy simultaneously with 'impressive' effect, then came the charge 'furious and frenzied'. Whilst the enemy resisted, the attack was not to use communication trenches, but to advance until the enemy works were conquered and then 'radiate' by means of patrols, and 'filter' through the enemy lines. Far from bypassing pockets of enemy resistance, 'no man capable of doing any damage' was to be left in the enemy forward positions.

Since it was 'impossible' for the staff to know whether or not a particular attack was successful very soon after the event, reserves should be pre-programmed and poured forward without waiting for intelligence to filter back. Indeed, 'one should push on fiercely in a preconceived and almost unintelligent manner till the moment when the last mesh is broken, otherwise it gets stronger before one's eyes and destroys one's greatest efforts'. Reserves were to operate with equal 'cool' to those who had gone before, regarding 'forming up under the pressure of danger' as 'a parade'. Nevertheless, reinforcements were to be in 'open' order with 'three or four' paces between each man.

Nothing less like fully developed *Stoss* or *Sturm* tactics could conceivably be imagined. The British translators of *L'Etude* certainly did not pretend that this was a model to be followed in all particulars, but offered the comment that it was the morale-raising element which justified bringing this possibly dubious analysis to a wider audience. As one commentator has put it, Laffargue 'looked back' as much as he looked forward, and for either those who wanted infiltration, or those who wanted mass attacks, justification was to be found in *L'Etude*. In fact, there is reason to suppose that even by September 1915 actual French practice in the field had advanced further in the direction of ad hoc formations, and at least 'shallow infiltration' methods, than Laffargue had suggested just a few months earlier. As a post-battle report of the German 23rd Infantry Regiment from that period recorded:

The first French attacking line consisted of a thin skirmish line equipped with hand grenades. As soon as this had reached our front line trenches, attacking columns in close order left the enemy's trenches. These consisted either of parties about 50 strong, formed in columns of fours, or irregular lines in close order. For purposes of close combat, the French were armed with bayonets and hand grenades. Whereas in the trenches the fighting was principally carried out with hand grenades, in the open country the bayonet was successfully employed by the companies of our regimental reserve during the counter-attack. Sections for bringing up material followed the enemy's attacking columns. The French showed remarkable skill and speed in consolidating the positions which they won. In places where we seriously threatened them, they offered little resistance and were soon prepared to give themselves up. Each French infantry company carried red and yellow flags into the attack with it, to act as indications to their own infantry and artillery of the newly won positions.

Certainly by the latter phases of Verdun less than a year later, the French use of non-linear formations and rapid salvoes of shelling were not much less advanced in their conception than the tactics which the Germans themselves were espousing.

Even more remarkably when we compare the German document *Proposals*, which slightly predates *L'Etude,* we find that most of the supposedly more novel features of Laffargue's appreciation are already present in German theory. These include the pushing forward of 'infantry guns', immediate capitalisation on success, breakthrough in one big attack (surprise as a 'crushing blow'), huge barrages directed partly at enemy reserves and batteries, and careful preparation. Moreover, *Proposals* is actually less prescriptive than the French document, though it still assumes that the first onslaught will be 'very strong' with companies coming on in four to six lines. Where possible, however, attacks were not to be delivered across wide stretches of No Man's Land, but shortened in time and distances by digging sap heads, or advancing by night and digging in close to the enemy. Rather than clearing every man themselves, the attacking waves would have 'special troops' detailed for clearing trenches and evacuating prisoners.

> The grenade is the principal weapon for use against an enemy in the trenches. Small obstacles must be crossed by the infantry unaided; pioneers will be responsible only for the more important works necessitating technical knowledge and equipment. The men should as far as possible be in light order: [leather] helmet, no pack, greatcoat, otherwise only ammunition and food.

Flame-throwers and Gas

It was also in 1915 that two weapons of great tactical promise for the breaking of trench lines made their debut: the flame-thrower and gas. Flame weapons had been known since antiquity, but it was only in the decade before the war that what we might recognise as the modern flame-thrower was perfected. Experiments by a *Landwehr* engineer company were conducted in mock defence of fortifications at Posen in 1907, and in 1910 a portable cylinder apparatus was patented by German inventor Richard Fiedler. In 1912 to 1913, under the direction of Captain Hermann Reddemann, the Posen fire department worked to help develop both a 'large' flame-thrower, which was mainly static, and a 'small' flame-thrower, which maintained significant tactical mobility. Whilst in its final form the large model boasted a 100-litre fuel tank and an impressive 45-metre range it was the *kleines-flammenwerfer* or *klief* model which ultimately had the most important impact, particularly in offensive operations. A fifty-man flame-thrower detachment, or *Flammenwerfer Abteilung,* led by Reddemann, was formed in January 1915. This would be one of three *Front Versuchstruppen der OHL* , or 'front line experimental units' created by Colonel Max Bauer of the General Staff at about this time, the other two being one of trench mortars under Major Lothes and the one under Major Kalsow for the testing of the 3.7cm 'assault cannon'. Bauer was unstinting in his appreciation of both Reddemann and Lothes, describing Lothes as a personal friend, about whom we might no doubt have heard more, were it not for his death at Verdun in 1916. Reddemann was similarly praised as a *'treue Mensch'* and a brave fighter.

The quite literal 'baptism of fire' of Reddemann's men came on 26 February at Malancourt near Verdun, and already there was a carefully worked-out tactical *modus operandi*. First, large flame-throwers were pre-deployed at a point where No Man's Land was narrow, and the attack was commenced with these being ignited, sending long gouts of flame into the enemy line. Unsurprisingly, the French had no immediate answer, so when small flame-throwers now accompanied the infantry advance the assault was a success in which the Germans suffered only moderate loss. On the receiving end, General Heymann, commanding 15th French Corps, observed that though burning was a fearful threat and that at one point a 'river of fire' formed in the bottom of the trenches, this was not actually the greatest danger. The thick, black smoke blinded the defenders and a few were suffocated, whilst the Germans were able to make use of this as cover. German machine guns also took advantage of the fact that some Frenchmen preferred to flee the smoke rather than be overcome. This trial by battle was accounted sufficient proof of utility for the enlargement of the unit under the patronage of the Crown Prince, which soon gained battalion strength as the Third Guard Pioneers.

Further flame attacks were made during 1915, one of which was reported by the rather despairing commander of the French 162nd regiment in the St. Hubert sector on 13 July:

> A thick black smoke was first observed, accompanied by a smell of pitch and tar. This smoke was driven forward by a favourable wind towards our trenches. At different points a jet of flame, the size of a man's forearm, then appeared, expanding as it approached our position. These flames descended either to the bottom of the trench, or to a depth of 50 cm, below the parapet, setting fire to the fascines or gabion revetment. The suddenness with which this new form of attack was made for the first time on 13th July, made it impossible for us to meet the attack. Up to the present no method has been discovered of combating the effect of these *Flammenwerfer*.

French Fifth Army Corps could offer no better advice at this time than to observe that some units had chosen to reduce their first line garrison to the minimum at the first sign that flame assault was imminent, and combat the attackers with rifles and machine guns from the second line.

Flame-thrower detachments were soon made a part of the new *Sturm* units, and by December 1915 a comprehensive set of instructions for the use of *Flammenwerfer* had been developed. At this time the Third Guard Pioneer Battalion numbered six companies, each of which possessed forty flame-throwers, about half of which were large, and half small. The new instructions specified that the large projectors of a company were to be deployed on a front of about fifty metres, the exact locations being selected by officers of the battalion on the basis of reconnaissance. Complete secrecy regarding the presence of *Flammenwerfer* was to be maintained, and the very word was not to be used either in orders or phone conversations, when a code device such as 'new mortars' or something similar was to be used. When the large weapons commenced the attack it was to be expected that the enemy in the opposing trenches would be:

> … destroyed or driven off, or if he happens to be in deep dugouts will have his morale so shaken that he will allow himself to be captured without resistance. Machine guns, even if provided with overhead cover or in block houses, are put out of action by directing flames against the loopholes. The flame attack lasts about one minute.

The assault by infantry and pioneers was to follow hard upon the big flame attack, being delivered no more than a minute later, thus taking advantage of the 'panic caused in the enemy's ranks'. The advance, preferably using fresh troops brought up for the purpose, would then be pushed through to the enemy's second or third line whenever possible. The attackers were best organised 'in four successive waves'. This assault party proper was to include: bombers, engineers and the small flame-throwers; a consolidating party for consolidation within the enemy lines; a communication trench construction party, to link the trenches captured back to the pre-existing German lines; and a carrying party whose duty was to bring forward material for obstacles and munitions. These groups were to gather quietly prior to the action in designated communication trenches and approaches, together with whatever loop-hole plates, sand bags, entrenching tools, signal pistols and ammunition were required. Also to be prepared in advance were short ladders – one for every three or four men of the assault party – to be used for a swift exit from the front-line trench. The men were to fix their bayonets before moving up to the front line, but carry their rifles at the trail whenever possible, avoiding unnecessary overcrowding. Attacking troops were to wear 'assault order', with greatcoat, tent sheet, mess tin, water bottle, four days' rations, two hundred rounds of ammunition and two hand grenades.

In cases where the attackers would have to traverse a German obstacle belt before reaching the enemy, this was to receive prior attention from the pioneers, who could cut parts of the wire the preceding night, or blow holes through which the men could pass ten to fifteen minutes before the actual assault.

> The assault is made immediately after the flame attack. The assault-
> ing party charges, followed closely by the consolidating party. The
> small flame projectors allotted to the assaulting party attack any
> machine guns that are still in action, blockhouses that are still being
> defended, etc., with short spurts of fire.

The men were to be instructed that there was no danger in attacking directly after the big flame attack because the fire extinguished
quickly, and small fires on the ground were not deemed a particular
hazard. Once within the enemy trench system the small flame projectors and bombers were to drive the enemy out to a 'considerable
distance' on either flank, and away down communication trenches,
and afterwards these avenues were to be sealed with sandbag bar-
ricades. Artillery and trench mortars were to provide supporting
fire for flame attacks, but were not to be used prior to the large
Flammenwerfer and thus spoiling the element of surprise. Rather,
they were to open fire as the infantry attack began. At this point
they would concentrate their fire on enemy rear areas, communication trenches, and adjoining sectors with the intention of isolating
the area under flame attack.

Thus it was that by the time of Verdun the flame-thrower units
had both the equipment and the tactical knowledge to take advantage of close co-operation with infantry assault units. Those who
fought nearby had cause to praise their efforts. A captain of the
117th Infantry Regiment watched a detachment, near Verdun,
'work over' a village with their flame jets. 'The *Flammenwerfer* soon
proved their worth', for in short order the French appeared 'wav-
ing their handkerchiefs', having given up the fight.

The flame attack gradually became part of most significant
assaults, and whilst only 15 such attacks were delivered in 1915,
this figure was increased to 160 in 1916, 165 in 1917, and 296 in the
last year of the war. In the meantime, the Guard Pioneers were
expanded to a complete three-battalion regiment, with twelve battle companies, a field trials company, and a training company; a
total establishment in excess of 3000 men. At the same time the
individual companies were rebalanced so that the small backpack
flame-throwers took precedence, with thirty or forty small weapons
and just twelve to fifteen large ones. The company was organised

into three platoons of five flame-thrower squads, one machine gun and one replacement squad. Each flame-thrower squad had two flame-throwers, whilst the machine gun squad had two light machine guns and a bomb thrower. Meticulous German record keepers would conclude that out of 653 flame attacks, 535 achieved success, against which just 118 had no useful result.

The use of flame-throwers required great courage, but their impact was quite limited in time and space, even though there were some fairly obvious tactical advantages that could readily be integrated into the infantry attack. Gas, on the other hand, appeared at first glance to have almost limitless potential, and was greeted by many as a wonder weapon, truly terrible and of great strategic importance. However, gas proved far more problematic to exploit productively, was very difficult to integrate with the infantry arm, and for a variety of reasons was ultimately used as gainfully by their enemies as by the Germans.

The gas cylinder attack by Major von Zingler's Pioneer Regiment Nr 35 near Ypres on 22 April 1915 has gone down in many text books as the 'first gas attack' and an act against the established rules of war, but this is something of an oversimplification. Gas *per se* was not ruled out by the Geneva Convention, but projectiles whose prime purpose was to kill, using gas, were. The result of this somewhat confused international agreement was that some nations eschewed gas altogether, but several experimented with it, either as an agent in projectiles intended to incapacitate rather than kill; or as a killing agent, but not in a projectile. This was rather tortuous logic, but all parties consoled themselves that they were adhering to the letter of the law, if being a little flexible with its spirit. The French used lachrymatory projectiles (to little or no effect) prior to April 1915; the Germans started to produce similar tear gas as early as the end of 1914, and had used poisoned gas shells at Bolimov on the Eastern Front (although, owing to the cold weather, these had failed to act properly). It would thus be more strictly accurate to call the gas release at the Second Ypres the first *fatal* gas attack. Though a local success, gas rapidly became a propaganda gift to the enemy. It also wrought novel horrors. As Rudolph Binding observed surveying the battlefield:

The effects of the successful gas attack were horrible. I am not pleased with the idea of poisoning men. Of course the entire world will rage about it first and then imitate us. All the dead lie on their backs with clenched fists; the whole field is yellow.

Whilst scientist in uniform Fritz Haber has been hailed, probably correctly, as the father of gas warfare, Colonel Max Bauer of the General Staff had a significant hand in its commissioning. It may fairly be said that this was one of the less well conceived and executed of the many projects with which he was involved. For though German industrial concerns such as Bayer, BASF and Hoechst were well placed to make toxic gas, getting it where it was wanted, and achieving battlefield results without dealing equal discomfort to one's own troops was a different matter. As if to prove the point, Haber and Bauer attended a gas test together at which they inadvertently rode into a gas cloud, and were lucky to escape with relatively minor injury. In setting up the first gas attack there were also other problems to overcome, not least of which was that many German generals did not wish to co-operate – though whether this was conservatism, or technical or moral scruple, is difficult to divine. Once the place of the attack had been identified almost 6,000 heavy cylinders had to be brought up for an attack frontage of just 7,000 metres. The enemy, who might have been adequately forewarned given better intelligence, broke and ran, but the German infantry exploiting this temporary advantage were ill prepared. Beyond advancing behind the cloud, there were as yet no special tactics. It was also the case that defending German soldiers against gas came low on the list of organisational priorities, with the result that few were given anything more effective than a face pad.

Interestingly, and contrary to popular expectation, gas did not prove to be a weapon of mass slaughter. In fact, relatively few of the victims of the new weapon actually died. Many were temporarily blinded, some suffered long-term health problems, but the vast majority survived and returned to active duty. Though new gases would be introduced over time, this picture of widespread injury, but few deaths, would change little since gas protection was regularly updated in a continuing race of attack and defence.

Before long the Allies were quite literally giving the Germans a taste of their own 'medicine'. This was made all the more bitter by the fact that on the Western Front, though the winds could blow in any direction, the prevailing currents were more often west to east than east to west. 'Blow back' was therefore a serious danger and German troops were at a natural disadvantage, both in the delivery of gas and in the soon-to-be escalating war of gas defence. The first German mask that could do a good job and be made and issued for the entire army appeared later during 1915. This *Gummi*, or rubberised fabric, mask was compact and fitted with eye pieces. It was initially stowed about the soldier's person in a bag, later up-rated to a metal cylinder. German gas instructions of early 1916 described the *Gummi* mask as follows:

> The anti-gas mask is made of gas-proof material into which are set two metal rings fitted with celluloid or 'cellone' windows to form gas-proof goggles. A third opening is fitted with a gas-tight 'breath filter', which is provided with a screw fitting closed with a rubber ring. By the side of each of the goggles there is a fold in the cloth for cleaning the glasses. The long tape is for suspending the mask [round the neck], the short elastic bands are for holding it on. The action of the mask depends on the fact that, by the passage of air through the filter, the irritant substances are retained [absorbed] by the contents. The anti-gas mask permits the wearer to speak and fight ... The 'drum' consists of a metal box which contains the absorbent material in the form of a slightly damp granular powder ... The mask and each drum are usually packed in separate tin boxes. A complete outfit consists of a canvas wallet with three [latterly two] tin boxes, of which the middle one contains the mask and directions for use, the two others each hold a breathing drum.

The German gas mask had several good points, also a number of negative ones. On the up side it had no trailing pipes, was fairly easy to use, and had a screw-in filter fixed direct to the face. It used only about twenty components. When new types of gas were introduced there was no need to scrap the whole mask – new filters could be devised and issued. Many of these same virtues became vices when new gases became so virulent, or were used at such concentrations, that small filters became inadequate. By 1917 the mask was therefore viewed as somewhat inferior. It could only be used for relatively limited periods, and to make matters worse, rubber was now virtually unobtainable. So it was that a new version of the mask was introduced, in leather, and the old and new ran in parallel, with the new gradually gaining ground as time progressed. The new mask was officially billed as a *wesentlicher Forschritt*, or 'considerable advance' but this was putting a happy gloss on necessity, for whilst it incorporated an ingenious arrangement of wires and the epidermis of a Bulgarian sheep, it was difficult to fit correctly. It was also prone to wear.

Specific orders on 'behaviour in gas attacks' were also included in the 1916 instructions. On gas being detected the alarm was to be raised immediately by sentries in the front-line post using 'appliances'. The alarm would be taken up by adjoining posts around. The manual writers probably assumed the provision of horns or bells, but contemporary photographs show everything from shell cases suspended to form impromptu gongs to the beating of frying pans. On hearing the alarm all personnel were to don their masks, fit them correctly and prepare any oxygen cylinders available so that casualties could quickly be given oxygen. Depending on local 'tactical conditions', different positions could be adopted by trench garrisons to maximise their safety. Those not needed in the trench could use dugouts, but these were to be made as air tight as possible using 'wetted curtains'. Following a gas attack and the repelling of any assault, the best way to purify dugouts was to open the entrances and light fires inside, which would warm the air and expel the gas.

The best statistics that we have regarding German gas casualties over the whole period of the war are that about 200,000 were in some way injured by gas, most being temporarily incapacitated. Of this admittedly large total only about 9,000 actually died, so the proportion of fatalities of those 'gassed' was less than five per cent. The total of German dead for the war was about two million, so those that were killed by gas were about half of one per cent.

The holistic approach that was used to address the tactical employment of the many weapons the infantry would encounter was initially nowhere to be seen. Gas cylinders were by nature very much weapons of chance. The pioneer opened the valves, and the gas went wherever the wind took it. Commands like 'cease fire' were useless once the evil genie was out of the bottle, and essentially the troops most at threat were those in the front line nearest the discharge – friend or foe. Enemy troops in the rear areas, reinforcements, gunners and senior officers were virtually immune if equipped with half-decent gas protection, as cylinder gas took time to arrive and was much dissipated by the time that it did. Just as counterproductive was the clumsiness of the cylinders. So difficult and dangerous was the task of installing them prior to discharge that it became usual practice to launch gas attacks in otherwise quiet sectors. Even here this was a difficult thing to accomplish quietly and secretly. Gas attacks therefore tended to become stereotyped and predictable, losing the key element of surprise. There was only one realistic answer to these problems: to get the gas on selected targets using projectiles; the very thing that had been explicitly banned under international agreement.

Nevertheless, German technologists now put considerable efforts into developing both mortar and artillery projectiles for gas delivery. From 1916 these became a significant factor. The important advantages were that gas could now be put on target, suddenly, without warning, and, rather than being a generalised front line curtain, it could be dropped on smaller areas such as batteries or movement corridors. Integration with the conventional bombardment in a way that was precise enough to be co-ordinated with the movement of troops on the ground became possible. Moreover, since by late 1916 the enemy (with the exception of the Russians) had distributed masks offering a high level of protection, it was accepted that gas would be widely used as a neutralisation weapon rather than a simple, if not very effective, killing agent. Complex gas shoots, often integrated with high explosives and smoke to produce a range of different effects as part of a fire plan, became known as *Buntschiessen* (coloured shoots) or *Buntkreuzschiessen* (coloured-cross shoots) owing to the range of colour-coded markings on the shells. Green crosses denoted phosgene and diphosgene, blue crosses arsenical compounds.

The new yellow cross was the symbol for so-called 'mustard gas'. Unlike many gases, it was accepted from the outset that mustard gas was essentially a weapon of harassment and wounding – a 'blistering agent'. On the statistical tables of death, mustard gas was in fact only more lethal than the old chlorine, and rather less injurious than agents such as chloropicrin, diphosgene and phosgene. Despite this, mustard gas shells were a weapon of tactical possibility, a stealthy and fiendish munition. Like most gas projectiles later in the war, they burst with a relatively modest 'plop', often indistinguishable over the roar of a bombardment. Since choking was not an early symptom, many initially failed to notice that they had been gassed until later, when their vision failed and huge blisters began to appear on any parts of the body that had been exposed to the gas. Relatively few enemy soldiers were actually killed, but this was not the point. Many were temporarily put out of action, medical facilities were dangerously stretched, and morale suffered as troops struggled around in masks having difficulty performing their tasks.

If there was a drawback to the new methods it was that gas projectiles had much smaller payloads than the big cylinders. A single 10.5cm 'blue cross' howitzer shell carried just 41g of the active chemical; a 'green cross' 7.7cm field gun round contained just over half a litre of gas in liquid form. The 21cm heavy projectile threw a far more respectable eight litres of liquid, but then the rate of fire was slower, and heavy *Morser* batteries were rarer and more valuable battlefield assets. The upshot of this was that to pacify a single square kilometre of enemy territory for a period of six to eight hours required 21,000 gas shells of various calibres. The only way around this troublesome statistic was to introduce a new mortar, or 'gas projector' that could be mounted in groups and fired huge shells at relatively low velocities, for the dedicated purpose of gas attacks. As British observers noted in 1918:

> A large number of these bombs, frequently several hundred, are discharged simultaneously against a small area. Sometimes the discharge is repeated. The discharge is accompanied by a sheet of flame and a loud explosion. The bomb in flight emits a trail of sparks and makes a loud whirring noise. It bursts with a loud detonation, producing a thick white cloud.

A single *Gaswerfer* bomb contained a healthy – unhealthy for the recipients – five litres of liquid. It was not, however, a novel idea:

the British Livens projector had come first and was arguably a more suitable weapon for the task, since the German device was unnecessarily complicated and wasted effort on accuracy, something scarcely necessary when large batteries were used.

Whatever the merits or demerits of gas warfare, the German army was thoroughly committed to its continuation. This is perhaps best illustrated by the fact that forward plans for 1919 suggested that it might be necessary for half of shell production to be gas rounds. For the infantry this meant that gas awareness, gas drills and advancing in co-ordination with gas shoots was an established part of the new tactics – though it was one over which the individual soldier would seldom have much control.

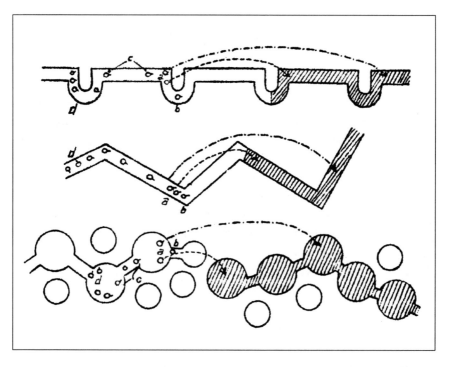

Methods for bombing along trenches, or from shell hole to shell hole, 1917. From the Austrian version of the German tactical manual.

4

Development of Defence

From the end of the great campaign at Verdun in the summer of 1916 to the spring of 1918 the German army in the West stood in an essentially defensive posture. One of the reasons that the Entente powers would continue to make so little progress here was that whilst – contrary to popular belief – they did experiment with new attacking methods, the Germans made equal or greater advances in the tactics of defence. In the process they would discard much of the theory contained in pre-war instructions, such as *Feld-Pionierdienst* 1911, and evolve new models for the use of both physical materials and human resources.

As in other fields, improvements to defence were not made overnight, but developed little by little. There was no sudden leap from crowded trenches to scattered pill boxes. Enemy methods were studied, and lessons were learned from previous battles. One of the earliest milestones was the document *Experiences Gained in the Winter Battle in Champagne,* prepared in April 1915 and issued the following month. As *Experiences* explained, it was based upon the methods of attack then used by the French against the German current positions. Hard facts and mistakes were not glossed over:

> The chief German trenches were, in order to obtain good command, generally sited on the forward slopes of the crest fairly high up, a fact which was of great assistance to the French artillery observers. The hostile artillery soon reduced our trenches to a condition in which they were little more than a mass of ruins, offering not a vestige of shelter. Successive attempts made by us during the night to repair the damage were rendered almost impossible by the massed fire

of trench mortars, rifle grenades and infantry; these attempts were responsible for our heavy losses, which were caused almost exclusively by artillery fire. Our losses were so serious that in many cases every living thing was annihilated, and all the obstacles completely destroyed, thus enabling the enemy's infantry to penetrate our positions with ease … The German artillery was entirely unable to combat the effects of the French artillery on our infantry. It is for consideration whether this want of success must be accepted as inevitable …

Quite how destructive artillery fire, and particularly high explosive rounds from howitzers, could be is difficult to describe to the uninitiated. German trench dwellers were soon using some evocative phrases which give us an inkling. One of the most familiar and widely used was *Trommelfeuer,* literally 'drum fire', in which the pummelling shells of a bombardment fell so thick and fast that their sound ran together like one great, deafening drum roll. When a man received a direct hit, or one near enough to tear him limb from limb, he might be described as turned to *Apfelsosse,* or 'apple sauce'. A soldier detailed to deal with the resulting fragments of humanity might need to 'scrape off' the victim, 'with a spoon and bury him in the pot'. One incident encountered by Ernst Jünger in the village of Fresnoy will suffice to indicate a horror which must have been replicated some thousands of times:

I lit a cigar and went into the smoke-filled cellar. In the middle of it there was a heap of wreckage – bedsteads, straw mattresses, and various pieces of furniture, all in fragments and piled nearly up to the roof. After we had put a few candles on ledges of the walls, we set to work. Catching hold of the limbs that stuck out from the wreckage, we pulled out the dead bodies. One had the head struck off, and the neck on the trunk was like a great sponge of blood. From the arm stumps of another the broken bones projected, and the uniform was saturated by a large wound in the chest. The entrails of the third poured out from a wound in the belly. As we pulled out the last a splintered board caught in the ghastly wound with a hideous noise. The orderly made a comment on this, and was reproved by my batman with these words: 'Best hold your tongue. In such matters talking nonsense serves no purpose'.

One of the most obvious lessons of early 1915 was that 'it [was] almost always impossible to hold a position with a single line of fire trenches'. Deep, fortified positions were indubitably better – those in the Champagne area reaching a thickness of about 2.5 kilometres by the time that *Experiences* was prepared. Whether the ideal trench system should occupy the highest ground available was a moot point, for command of the surrounding territory brought with it the equal danger of destruction by shell fire. Conversely, the use of reverse slopes was safer from bombardment, but would mean that the opposition could take up the forward slope whilst important observation points were sacrificed. Either way, short fields of fire for the defending infantry were not usually found to be a serious handicap. What was more significant was this realisation:

> … we have learnt by experiment and experience that what was required was not one or even several lines of fixed defences, but rather a fortified zone which permitted a certain liberty of action, so that the best use could be made of all the advantages offered by the configuration of the ground, and all the disadvantages could as far as possible be overcome.

Within such a network, the defenders would be well advised to pick the point that they considered the 'tactical key'. Here a transverse trench could be designated as the 'main line of defence'. This was to be so dug as to be, as far as possible, out of sight of enemy observation, for example: just behind a crest or in woods. Out from the main trench towards the enemy were communication trenches, linking to the forward fire trenches or *Schutzengraben*. Also in this front area would be machine gun posts, observation posts and listening stations. Further back, behind the main position, additional trenches could be prepared either before or during a battle to form stop lines or 'cul-de-sacs' into which enemy units might blunder should they succeed in getting through the main line. These and other positions would be accessible from rear areas through communication trenches. Dummy batteries and infantry positions were also to be established wherever possible, confusing enemy observers and dissipating the effects of shelling and assaults.

Experiences also marked a stage in the reduction of the numbers of men in a given trench line in order to reduce casualties whilst increasing the role of tactically sited machine weapons:

> The construction of flanking works and obstacles is by far the most important item. It is impossible to have too many of these works. They enable a position to be defended by very reduced forces with a very restricted field of fire and even in case of complete surprise. Machine guns are particularly well adapted for flanking purposes, as are guns which are well concealed from the enemy. Flanking is rendered possible from the fire trenches themselves by means of a tenaille or bastion trace or from advanced positions.
>
> It should be possible to subject these to flanking fire from the rear or better still to cross fire. Obstacles, as we have learnt by experience, are completely destroyed by methodical artillery fire. They should consequently be concealed from view, divided into parallel lines, and their height kept as low as possible; further they should be provided with iron posts, with base pieces securely anchored, and obstacles which can be rapidly placed in position should be held in readiness.
>
> In order to watch both the ground in front and the obstacles, rifle pits must be constructed in front of the trenches, which can be reached by crawling along shallow trenches. For frontal defence, loopholes should be provided with steel shields, but it should also be possible to fire over the parapet.

Ideally, trench garrisons were to be provided with shelters, the emphasis being on having many small shelters for the troops providing the different battle functions within the defensive area. According to the best plan, each front-line trench squad was to have its own dugout 'covered with three metres of earth and with two entrances for the occupants of each trench'. Troops acting in support were similarly to have their own cover, close by and connected to the front fire positions by communication trench. Shelters for reserves, further to the rear, were likewise to be connected by communication trenches. In this way it would be possible for the trench garrison to retire under cover during heavy bombardment. Similarly, reserves would be able to proceed from the rear areas to the front-line trenches without sacrificing protection.

The difficulties of taking such a labyrinth were by no means underestimated, and again it was the roles of grenades and machine guns that were stressed in trench fighting:

> It must be recognised that in the present trench warfare, deep, narrow trenches, with numerous traverses and salients, provide cover which enables the defenders to hold a position with unprecedented obstinacy when fighting at close quarters, but which makes it extremely difficult to direct the fighting. In this kind of warfare hand grenades are almost the only weapon which can be used, since they alone, when thrown into keeps [strong points], kill the enemy and force him to evacuate a position. Hand grenades are not only the chief offensive weapon, but are also, in conjunction with rifles and machine guns, an effective weapon of defence, since they can be thrown from a trench, or, should the enemy succeed in penetrating the position, be thrown at him over the traverses. During night operations, hand grenades can be used with advantage on open ground.

Another problem for the attacker, perhaps not immediately apparent at first glance, was that fire trenches had a front and a back, being constructed for the convenience of a garrison facing towards enemy positions. Troops jumping into a trench from the front might therefore find themselves in great difficulty facing a counter-attack from the enemy rear area. Fire steps would be lacking, observation would be poor, and loopholes pointed in the wrong direction. One of the first tasks of a successful attack force was therefore to 'reverse the parapets of the captured trench' and to 'reconstruct the trench itself so that he can fire towards the enemy'. For a force which had just been through the trauma of an attack 'over the top' – at least tired, if not decimated by the battle – this was far easier said than done. It also necessitated a ready supply of tools if it was to be managed in any reasonable time frame. As long as this had not been achieved, the newly taken area was vulnerable to counter-attack which might well eject the occupier. When troops that had entered an enemy trench managed to consolidate their hold, they could still be an isolated force at a disadvantage against a determined defender. So it was that German forces were instructed to make simultaneous attacks down the trench from the ends and across the open ground from the rear, catching the attackers in a pincer. Such considered counterstrokes might be supported onto target by artillery, mortars and rifle grenades. Even if this failed to dislodge the opposition, the defence could then resort to 'sapping and mining operations', digging their way back into their old lines.

A particularly important point noted in *Experiences* was that weapons pointed directly at the enemy front from right angles, or even trenches themselves, were not crucial to the defence of a position as long as the ground between two points in a defensive area was swept by enfilading fire:

> An attack over open ground, even for very short distances (300 metres and less) can be rendered practically impossible by enfilade fire from a single gun or machine gun; the absence of frontal defences and even the absence of obstacles does not make much difference.

This apparently casual observation would have important ramifications for the development of defensive tactics over the next two years. For if it was weapons positioned so as to sweep the ground which really mattered, then continuous trench lines might one day be rendered relatively unimportant – superfluous even – to a defended locality.

The immediate lesson, however, was that defence in depth promised the greatest protection, reducing casualties whilst catching the enemy in a bullet-swept web of ditches and wire that he could only fight his way out of with the bloodiest of efforts. To this end, the German High Command ordered that a second or reserve line should be constructed between two to three kilometres behind the existing 'first line' along its entire length. The French sector received the highest priority, since it was here that the attacks were currently the strongest. The doubling of the line against the British came soon after, in parallel with the build up of numbers of enemy troops. The lesson of the particular was thus applied to the whole. Some heavily contested areas already had two or even three lines, but to dig hundreds more kilometres of trench and establish massive new belts of wire was still a colossal undertaking. The job would be completed by the end of 1915. Solid defence in the West would allow attack in the East, and ultimately that assault would be successful. Little wonder that popular patriotic postcards would refer to the bastion of the Western Front as *Die Gottesmauer* : 'God's wall'.

Practical experience from the Champagne in the autumn of 1915 was used to add further new details to the German defensive doctrine. Perhaps most important were adjustments to the dispositions of units within trench systems. According to von Below's 2nd Army instructions, it was now customary for each regiment to defend its sector by means of defence in depth over a relatively narrow front. Of its twelve basic companies, just four would be put in the front line trenches, and each of these would hold three to six hundred metres of front. Four more were put in position further back as 'support', whilst the remainder were well behind the front line in regimental or brigade reserves. However, keeping such reserves in the cellars of destroyed villages was proved to be impractical, as gathering them in enough time to be of use was impossible. The regimental back stop was therefore now ordered to occupy either 'the rearmost trenches of the first line system' or an 'intermediate line' – which of course had the impact of making the trench systems of a defensive front thicker still.

All the available data seemed to suggest indeed that more thinly held, but distributed in greater depth, was the way to go. Even 'a weak garrison' generally proved enough to bring an attacking enemy to a halt in the front line. Here he could be engaged by men in the support positions as well as by 'well-placed machine guns' and 'emergency garrisons' held in the vicinity of the communication trenches. These last could find men for 'strong bombing parties' who would move up the trench to the aid of the front line when required. How to prevent the men in the first fire trench from being surprised after a bombardment remained a matter of debate. One school of thought recommended that an 'adequate' garrison be maintained in the foremost trench, and these should be kept under cover to spring to the parapet as soon as an alarm was sounded or the bombardment lengthened. The numbers of these men could be reduced in accordance with the availability of enfilading fire from machine guns and other troops. The other school of thought was that a number of sentries was required to keep watch from posts. In either case, the responsibility now devolved upon squad or *Gruppe* leaders and even the individual soldier, to realise that it was up to them to 'know that the success or failure of the defence depends entirely on the timely manning of the parapet'. In some instances, it appears that local commanders were already taking the unilateral decision to rely on sentries alone in the front line *Schutzengraben*. They would then pour men back into the line as soon as the barrage ceased, or enemy attack was confirmed. The command of 2nd Army frowned upon this tactic, ordering that holding the front line trenches was 'absolutely to be adhered to'. So it was that front-line innovation, in this instance as in so many others, prefigured official adoption and subsequent absorption into new doctrine.

Communication failures continued to be a serious problem to defenders as well as to attackers. Where the usual channels failed, two relatively basic expedients were to be used to rectify the problems as best as possible. The first of these was the simple and very ancient idea of the runner:

> The telephone connections forward from the regiment and battalion were for the most part cut. The surest means of communication proved to be daring, reliable men, who worked their way backwards and forwards from shell hole to shell hole. The provision of some special means of recognition (arm band) for these men proved to be of value. Otherwise they were often held back by officers in the front line and used for other purposes.

This mention of 'special' recognition no doubt explains the surviving photographs of German soldiers wearing a large 'M' on an arm band, *Meldungen* meaning reports or dispatches, *Meldeganger* being a messenger or runner.

Another imperfect but widely used and innovative solution to poor communications was for the front-line infantry to give simple signals direct to the artillery by means of *Leucht* or flare pistols. This seemingly obvious measure met with a number of objections in that it circumvented the established chains of command, and led to the wasting of shells by nervous infantry officers. It was also imperfect in that in the confusion of battle, flares might be misinterpreted, go unseen, or get mixed up with similar devices used by the enemy. Even so, for battles of fixed positions where simple signal codes could be established in advance, the idea had much to recommend it. The concept was also an important small step on the way to fuller infantry–artillery co-ordination, and the synchronisation of infantry needs with artillery resources. Signal lamps and pigeons would also see use, with radio eventually gaining in quality and significance towards the end of the war, but no successful man-portable set would see use prior to November 1918.

Barbed wire, a rarity in 1914, was plentiful by 1916. No longer were a few strands, perhaps adorned with tin cans for early warning, accounted as anything like sufficient. As a British intelligence document pointed out, German wiring techniques were now highly sophisticated, and properly established belts of wire assumed their own tactical significance:

> One of the most distinctive features of the German defences is the labour expended on constructing thoroughly good and effective wire entanglements. Every defensive line, switch and strong point, is protected by a strong wire entanglement on iron or wooden posts, sited, if possible, so as not to be parallel to the trenches behind it. Endeavours are made to provide two or three belts, each 10 to 15 feet or more deep, with an interval between the belts of 15 to 30 feet. These intervals are filled, if possible, with trip wires, pointed iron stakes etc., and blocked by occasional bands of entanglement connecting the belts. Four different lengths of iron screw picket are supplied, the longest, which has five loops, giving a height of four feet above ground. The distance apart of the pickets in an entanglement is intentionally irregular, but averages about 6.5 feet.
>
> Knife rests, expanding cylinders of wire, and other portable obstacles are used when it is impossible to erect posts. A special portable obstacle, called the Lochmann entanglement, has sometimes been used. It consists of a net of barbed wire, about 13 feet wide and 180 feet long, which is unrolled and then erected on two legged iron pickets, placed by men who crawl under the wire and peg it down at the sides. If possible, entanglements are protected from the enemy's artillery fire by placing them in natural depressions or in sheltered trenches dug for the purpose. This is to be expected in the second or third positions, rather than in the front system.

Despite best efforts on the part of German defenders, artillery, in ever increasing amounts, firing ever heavier shells, caused greater proportions of the casualties. One German estimate suggested that late in the war as many as eighty per cent of fatalities were caused by shells. Barrages certainly caused some of the most brutal dehumanisation. Many soldiers were separated temporarily, or permanently, from their wits. The physical effects were even worse, as was observed by former law student Hugo Muller, looking at the dead near Arras:

> Lucky the few whom we or those opposite have been able to inter with some sort of decency – for fragments of human bodies are still hanging in the barbed wire. Only a little while ago, close in front of our trench, was a human hand with a ring on one finger; a few yards away was a forearm, of which only the bone remained – so good does human flesh taste to rats! Ghastly! The man who could never shudder and shake would learn how here!

On both sides the idea that more and more shells were the answer to the tactical dilemma of unbreachable trench lines, became well established by late 1915. Amongst the French, both Foch and Pétain were quoted as being of the opinion that it was now artillery which cleared the ground; infantry occupied it. In the middle war period similar preconceptions would be applied by the British, especially where troops were thought to be insufficiently well trained to fight in other ways. At Verdun under General von Falkenhayn, artillery was intended play the key role in inflicting 'the utmost injury' on the enemy; in a battle which he subsequently protested was never seriously intended as a 'breakthrough operation'. As he put it: 'an extraordinary amount of artillery' was devoted to the purpose, together with stocks of shells exceeding 'all previous experience'. That such expectations of success by guns would be so cruelly shattered was at least in part due to the fact that counter-artillery preparations and defensive plans kept pace with the new offensive ideas and technology.

As the Germans were mainly on the defensive until the end of 1915, many commentators have noted correctly the progressive and systematic thinning and the deepening of the German lines at this period. Though it may be argued with some justification that they were quickest off the mark, the maximum length of time between

German innovation and Allied imitation was no more than a few months. As was so often the case, one side copied the other, or learned quickly by mistakes in the face of the enemy. So it was that as early as February 1916 German intelligence had realised that the French and then the British had already abandoned the policy of defending the front line 'at all costs'. Though there were differences in detail, all combatants in the west were now relying on a form of defence in depth, and the German assault at Verdun would meet anew many of the problems that the Allies had struggled with over the preceding months. In the simple, brutal terms of the butcher's bill, the German Army did better proportionately than their Allied adversaries had done earlier, which suggests a greater tactical sophistication, but it was only a matter of degree, for the better part of 100,000 German soldiers died at Verdun, with at least another 200,000 wounded.

New materials, at first sought out for their durability, strength or suitability to supplement existing stores, also began to take on a wider defensive significance from the end of 1915. The story of reinforced concrete on the Western Front is a particularly important instance. Although such detail may at first glance appear mundane, ultimately, the widespread adoption of the pill box would have great tactical impact. Following smaller-scale experiments, the barging of large volumes of basalt and gravel down the Rhine from Germany began in the latter part of 1915. Much of the material intended for new defence works was quarried from the rock of Western Germany, and some came from captured French and Belgian cement works. Amazingly, use was also made of British Portland Cement which had been exported to the Netherlands and later redirected. The materials were sourced and checked for their appropriateness to the project by teams of geologists, *Geologen Stelle*, attached to army corps and divisions.

Initially, it appears that the main driving forces behind the use of concrete and steel reinforcement were not to invent new defences and tactics, but to solve existing problems. One major difficulty to which reinforced concrete offered a solution was in preventing the collapse of dugouts and entrances. All too often, deep, covered positions had protected their occupants reasonably well until either a heavy high-explosive shell had scored a direct hit, or a projectile landing nearby had blocked the entrance with earth. Groups of men had thus been put out of action by a single unlucky round. Arches and entrances of concrete were constructed in places, but a simpler and more effective remedy was to build a reinforced slab over all, or part, of the work to be protected, and layer it with chalk, earth, and wood as available. The concrete thus formed a course, or courses, within a larger construction that burst shells on impact, the blast and debris from which was caught and muffled in the other, softer layers.

Another problem reinforced concrete could help with was that, particularly in Flanders, parts of the front were very low-lying and close to the water table. Digging too deep merely produced flooded trenches which were virtually impossible to pump out. Building up breastworks in the regulation manner was useful, but tended to produce large, obvious and not terribly shell-resistant barriers in the landscape. Lack of overhead cover meant that mortars and howitzers could create havoc amongst breastworks. The obvious answer appeared to be to build up rather than down, and to use materials capable of forming a strong overhead defence as well as some protection against a direct hit. Economy of materials, and difficulties of concealment, dictated that concrete was not generally used to line entire trenches, but to make smaller structures similar to the pre-existing idea of the 'blockhouse'.

The new concrete stand-alone bunker would be described in German as *Mannschafts Eisenbeton Unterstand*, which translates as 'team (or personnel) reinforced concrete shelter'. Understandably, the acronym *MEBU* was soon found more felicitous, though to British troops these monstrosities looked more like giant medicine containers – or 'pill boxes'. Some of the German concrete works did feature machine gun embrasures or rifle ports, but many did not. The logic behind this was that the majority served essentially as temporary shelter from shelling, and that the garrison was intended to dash out into nearby shell holes, trenches or pits, or even mount their machine gun to fire over the top of the bunker when the enemy infantry advanced. Reducing the number of holes through the surface of the *MEBU* increased its structural integrity, decreased complexity of construction and ultimately improved cover from shell fire. However, the lack of provision for the garrison to see out could cause problems when the enemy succeeded in reaching the position unobserved, and managed to capture the occupants by the simple expedient of covering the entrance with a rifle and threatening to throw in grenades.

Part of the answer to such tactics was to mix concrete-covered observation posts with shelters and machine gun bunkers, improving the warning system and covering friendly positions with fire from other localities. Another was to make each bunker as difficult to locate as possible. Whilst surviving German structures in the Belgian and French landscape are usually obvious, standing like sugar cubes against the brown earth and green fields, few would have looked like this when they were first constructed. Many incorporated a bank of earth on one or more faces; some were built into existing farm walls; others were covered with bundles of wood or foliage; a few made use of paint or texturing. As a Royal Engineer's report noted:

> ... to conceal concrete works, mortar is plastered on the surface before the cement has set, and on this moss or roots and weeds are thrown and stamped in on the chance of their growing. In some cases the concrete has merely been painted with large irregular patches of different colours.

Behind the front line, pill boxes could also be designed with cosmetic features such as pitched roofs or window frames suggesting a shed or barn.

Constructing large numbers of concrete structures, some of them close to the enemy line, caused numerous practical difficulties. Not least of these was keeping large quantities of cement dry on the waterlogged battlefield until they were needed. One solution was the provision of *Mischplatze* , or 'mixing places' further back, and moving up the ready-prepared wet cement as swiftly as possible on miniature tram lines. From early 1916 another answer was the use of precast blocks. These were moulded like giant bricks with holes through them, then moved into position where they were laid and reinforced using bars pushed through the holes, and fixed with cement and sand mortar.

Effective as they were, occupying pill boxes under fire was no picnic – as Lieutenant Wimberley of the Machine Gun Corps discovered inside a German fortification at Ferdinand Farm on the Menin Road:

> It had very thick concrete walls but it was a curious sort of place to have a headquarters. It had been built by the Germans, and so the entrance faced the German lines. Inside it was only about five foot high and at the bottom was about two foot of water. This water was simply horrid, full of refuse, old tins and even excreta. Whenever shells burst near it the smell was perfectly overpowering. Luckily there was a sort of concrete shelf the Boche had made about two foot above ground level. It was on this shelf that four officers and six other ranks spent the night. There wasn't room to lie down, there was hardly room to sit upright, and we more or less crouched there. Outside the pillbox was an enormous shell hole full of water, and the only way out was over a ten inch plank. Inside the shell hole was the dead body of a Boche who had been there a very long time and who floated or sank on alternate days according to the atmosphere.

Whilst the theory of strongpoints and bunker defence was still in its infancy, in mid 1916 the battle of the Somme would provide a fresh, if not welcome, crop of data from which the theorists could begin to formulate the next generation of defence instructions. Though huge losses were inflicted on the British infantry, enemy artillery made the most forceful impression on German troops and tacticians alike. Whilst light shells scattered shrapnel, the heavy high-explosive types made great excavations which blew upwards huge quantities of earth, stones and debris, which fell back 'like rain'. As *Leutnant* Ernst Jünger of the 73rd Fusiliers recalled, there was a zone of a kilometre where explosives held absolute sway:

> It was the days at Guillemont that first made me aware of the overwhelming effects of the *Materialschlacht* [war of material]. We had to adapt ourselves to an entirely new phase of war. The communications between the artillery and the liaison officers were utterly crippled by the terrific fire. Despatch riders failed to get through the hail of metal, and telephone lines were no sooner laid than they were shot to pieces ... Every hand's breadth of ground had been churned up again and again; trees had been uprooted, smashed and ground

into matchwood, the houses blown to bits and turned to dust; hills had been levelled.

Heavy casualties were, so he thought, the result of an old Prussian obstinacy, that the line was being held at all costs, with more and more battalions thrown forward into trenches that were already 'overmanned'.

First Army Headquarters went so far as to send questionnaires to its subordinate commands, seeking out specific categories of information on the success or otherwise of current techniques. These were then modified in accordance with current conditions. Ironically, quite a lot of this intelligence would find its way back to the British in the form of the translated document *Lessons Drawn From the Battle of the Somme by Stein's Group*. Amongst these lessons were that the regimental sectors of the trench systems were still too wide, and still not deployed in great enough depth. Since artillery caused the greatest number of casualties, dugouts were identified as crucial, it now being intended that their numbers be increased until 'there are sufficient to accommodate the infantry garrison which the Division considers necessary for the repulse of a prepared attack'. The depth of these dugouts, in earth, was to be anything from six to eight metres for combat teams, and greater, if possible, for medical, telephone and kitchen bunkers. Machine guns were vulnerable if left on the surface in anything but 'very strong concrete emplacements'. Accordingly, the standard drill was to take the weapons below ground during bombardment, later replacing them 'rapidly in position at suitable points on the parapet', without making use of the standard 'sledge mounts', which were found to be 'too heavy for trench warfare'. The British provision of 'light' Lewis guns was especially problematic, these being 'brought into action very quickly and skilfully in newly captured positions. It is very desirable that our [German] infantry should be equipped with a large number of light machine guns of this description in order to increase the intensity of its fire'.

The cumulation of knowledge gathered during 1915 and 1916 was ultimately published as a universal instruction in the form of the new manual. This was *Stellungsbau, the Manual of Position Warfare For All Arms: Part I, The Construction of Field Defences*, issued by the Prussian War Ministry, November 1916. The three guiding principles were not essentially original, being: economy of forces; diminution of friendly losses and increase of enemy losses; and utilisation of the ground in such a manner as to give favourable conditions for combat, whilst denying these to the enemy. How this was actually to be achieved had, however, changed a great deal since 1914. Long and unobstructed fields of fire were no longer considered particularly significant. More important was that artillery-observation posts should be provided and protected, whilst main defensive lines were best placed on reverse slopes with only short fields of fire. Front-line trenches were similarly best kept out of view, the only reasonable excuse for not doing so being that of artillery observation. Equally, trenches themselves were no longer the be all and end all of the defence lines, since 'machine gun posts and dugouts form the framework of all infantry fighting lines'. Machine guns could make do with fields of fire restricted to as little as a hundred metres, and should be concealed in emplace-ments, enfilading obstacles such as wire and gaps between the lines and zones. Not many would actually be positioned in the front line itself, but those that were could be made more effective by moving them around.

Flimsy, 'splinter-proof' constructions were not really worth bothering with. Dugout planners were now to concentrate on more substantial works, which were either shell- or bomb-proof, the former being capable of resisting projectiles of up to 150mm, the latter 'continuous shelling' from 200mm guns and single hits from even heavier calibres. Ideally, front-line shelters were to be kept relatively shallow, but well protected by means of reinforced concrete. From these, small garrisons could reach the fire steps of nearby trenches very quickly. In the rearmost lines, dugouts could be larger and deeper, though the further this trend progressed the more necessary it would be to have multiple exits, and, where pos-sible, tunnels from communication trenches to dugouts were to be provided. These larger dugouts could contain one or two *Gruppe* and a leader, being anything up to nineteen men.

Though it had hitherto been recommended that trenches should be narrow and deep for good cover, it was now recognised that they were inconvenient for traffic and quickly blocked by falls of earth. To this end, communication trenches in particular were now ordered to be:

... deep and broad, with sides not too steep; all earth thrown up should be kept low, and separated from the trenches by wide berms. The revetting of trenches should be limited, for the amount of labour involved is out of all proportion to the utility. Too much attention to keeping trenches neat and tidy is forbidden. The labour necessary is better devoted to new work ... All fire, communication and approach trenches should be carefully marked with coloured sign boards, sign posts, etc.

Importantly, *Stellungsbau* recognised that successful defence did not consist in blindly protecting every metre of ground equally, but that sectors should be carefully planned and held so that withdrawal from parts of the position did not endanger the whole. The position would of course be planned to take full advantage of natural features. The 'strongly constructed' first position was to be 'close up to the enemy', doubtless making it difficult for the opposition to hit it with the full power of its bombardment without endangering their own troops. This first position would itself have 'plenty of depth', being several continuous but not parallel (and therefore obvious) lines. Communication trenches to the rear were to be copious, indeed they could never be 'too numerous'. One or more rearward positions were to be so placed that no bombardment could simultaneously hit both – the total depth of the defensive zones might therefore be anything up to ten kilometres. The back stop itself did not need to have as many lines of trenches as the first line. An important emphasis was put upon the idea of 'strong points' and smaller 'holding points', both between the positions and behind the rearmost position. The strong points might be villages or copses, whilst holding points could be as small as shell craters, odd ruins, thickets, hedges, and short trenches. It was hoped that in the long term, strong points might themselves be joined by continuous trenches, forming another line. The improvement of defences was to be continuous, 'even during a battle'.

As far as the defending troops were concerned, an adequate garrison of troops and machine guns was required in the front rank to deal with 'any surprise attacks', but the bulk of the manpower was to be accommodated in the rearmost lines. Reserves were to be positioned so as to make it difficult for enemy assault troops to spread out, and eventually those penetrating too far would find themselves 'encircled on front and flank by fire trenches and obstacles, and then it should be possible to annihilate him with well-hidden machine guns'. This was no linear plan but a defended area. The defence itself was not to be purely passive, but endowed with *Schlagfertigkeit*, 'quick wittedness' – or a readiness to strike back. Irregularity and unpredictability were the keys to the positioning of both obstacle zones and heavy weapons. Wire was to be laid out in multiple belts with gaps between them, not in regular lines. Trench mortar positions had been constructed deep and strong, but on balance a greater number of weaker positions was more desirable, thus giving an element of surprise and causing the enemy to expend effort on empty mortar pits. Artillery batteries near to the front were best given screens or emplacements, and dugouts for the crews, but the layout of such positions was not to be neat and regular, providing an easy target. Battery positions were to have their own obstacles and provision for close defence, but nothing that could give them away to aerial observers.

The British intelligence document *Summary of Recent Information Regarding the German Army and its Methods*, which appeared in January 1917, added a number of interesting observations on defensive tactics, not least on the use of snipers. In the usual German system, snipers were not detailed to a particular post or loophole, but to a certain section of trench. On this sector a number of loopholes would be prepared in advance, this multiplication being favoured 'as it gives an enemy a large number to keep under observation, without requiring many snipers to man them'. Such loopholes varied considerably in design and complexity, the simplest being merely small gaps between sandbags, a loophole plate concealed in the parapet, or one or more holes cut into a tree or stump. Coils of wire, discarded tin cans and coloured sand bags were all used to confuse observers as to where loopholes emerged. On occasion snipers moved into positions in front of the main line, as for example shell holes where loophole plates and supplies of food might make longer-term occupation practicable. In certain instances, these independent snipers might be left behind after the main garrison had withdrawn, inflicting disproportionate casualties before they could be detected. Perhaps the most elaborate sniper post encountered consisted of a 'stoutly framed, rectangular, wooden sentry box, about 6 feet high and 4 feet square, placed in a recess in a parapet'. The roof of such a post consisted of planks, corrugated iron, steel rails or plates, covered with earth against external observation. On the inside of the post was concealed a steel loophole plate, and a clamp to hold a rifle. Being adjustable horizontally and vertically, this allowed the sniper to home in accurately on an enemy gap in the trench line, or observation post, and would have minimised the fatigue that snipers often experienced in waiting for targets to appear.

By mid 1917 the theory of flexible defence based upon a deep web of posts and weapons positions, rather than one or more lateral trenches, was fully developed. It was in Flanders where it would find its most pure practical expression, owing at least in part to the obvious practical difficulty of creating elaborate trench systems in waterlogged ground. As Jünger explained in *Das Waldchen 125*:

> It will be proved to the hilt, that if the war goes on, that whether in attack or defence, fighting can only be done in zones. But we must at the same time manage to rid ourselves once and for all of the disastrous idea of the line with which history and the drill yard have saddled us all through the war.

The best simile, to his mind, was that of 'a net into which the enemy may certainly penetrate here and there, but where he will at once be overwhelmed from all sides by a web of fire'. The ground would be held not shoulder to shoulder 'but isolated from one another in small groups and distributed far and wide over the smoking country, conductors of elemental forces'.

It is commonly accepted that the two characters to whom most credit is due for the ultimate evolution of the new system of 'elastic defence' were General Fritz von Lossberg, and *Oberst* Max Bauer of the General Staff – though as we have seen, there was plentiful input from others, and the change took two and a half years of progressive modification. Indeed, there is evidence to suggest that Lossberg was originally a devotee of greater rigidity, and that a mixture of practical experience gleaned from enemy attacks and dialogue with Bauer converted him to become the prime exponent of the new ideas. As the emphasis changed, there were even times when memorandums circulated containing both recommendations for rigidity and greater flexibility. By January 1917 the 'deep and flexible' school of thought, in which 'zones' were paramount, had won the theoretical argument. The orthodoxy was now part eight of the manual of position warfare, *The Principles of Command in the Defensive Battle*. Now more than half of the available troops would be held back behind the battle zone; the remainder would be split between the 'forward' zone and the more-important 'battle zone' where the real action was expected to happen. The key to defence would be *Eingriff* ('alert') divisions which would thrust forward from the rear at vital moments to hit attackers who had exhausted themselves wading through the forward defence.

Yet the heaviest burden of the defence was not now on the 'big battalions', but on sections – the smallest organisational groups who were expected to carry on working even when cut off by the battle from the outside world. As Hindenburg himself pointed out:

> Our new defensive system made heavy demands on the moral resolution and capacity of the troops because it abandoned the firm external rigidity of the serried lines of defence, and thereby made the independent action, even of the smallest bodies of troops, the supreme consideration. Tactical co-operation was no longer obtained by defences that were continuous to the eye, but consisted of the invisible moral bond between the men engaged in such tactical co-operation. It is no exaggeration to say that in these circumstances the adoption of the new principles was the greatest evidence of confidence which was placed in the moral and mental powers of our army, down to its smallest unit.

To turn theory into a practice which the army understood and would operate as second nature, however, took some months to inculcate. To do so, the General Staff used both 'trickle-down' methods and 'schools' of a type familiar to the British. A key figure in the dissemination of the new learning was General Otto von Moser, an experienced front-line commander who had previously been wounded. His new command was a 'testing and instructional' division, which would both conduct experiments in the assimilation of the ideas, and teach them on as wide a scale as possible. For senior officers, von Moser instituted a *Divisonskommandeur-Schule*, a school for divisional-level officers running a week-long course. Three cohorts put through the course during February and March 1917 broke the back of the task, and Moser's work was made easier by the support of officers seconded from the General Staff, including *Hauptmann* Geyer.

Perhaps the ultimate expression of defensive flexibility, and the understanding that crude areas of ground were not the sole measure of success, was the retreat in the West to the Siegfried line (known to the opposition as the 'Hindenburg' line) during March 1917. This retirement, as Hindenburg noted in his memoirs, 'not only gave us more favourable local conditions on the Western Front, but improved our whole situation. The shortening of our lines in the West made it possible for us to build up strong reserves'. Retreats, however explained, did not go down well with the German public, but since the ground given up had been captured from the enemy in the first place it was politically possible. Part of the comparative inflexibility of the French and British in this respect must be put down to the fact that any step backwards on their part would be abandoning yet more of France, or the little that remained of Belgium, to the enemy.

Efficient as this German posture was, the new tactics of defence were not introduced entirely without mishap. Some senior officers were slow to learn; others doubted the premise; some were reluctant to relinquish the control needed to allow counter-attacks to be mounted on the initiative of subordinates. At least as often, there were problems caused by lack of resources; divisions which, in theory, would mount swift counterattacks from reserve positions sometimes were not there – sometimes did not even exist. During the battle of Arras, and even at times during the Third Ypres, both new and older methods would be used. Moreover, new lessons were also learned in the face of enemy innovations, such as improving tanks, limited 'bite and hold' attacks, and better artillery techniques and improved projectiles, both gas and conventional. At Cambrai in particular, Hindenburg would be taken aback by the 'brilliant initial success' of tanks. Before the end of the year the German defenders had added yet another trick to the repertoire:

pulling back a few hundred yards as soon as a major attack was apparent. This meant that No Man's Land was effectively much wider. Some of the enemy barrage would now fall into empty space, merely churning up the ground in front of their own troops, whilst German guns had a bigger area that they could hit without endangering their own infantry.

By 1918 the tactics of the German defensive battle had changed out of all recognition, as Ludendorff explained:

> I attached great significance to what I learned about our infantry at Cambrai, about their tactics and preparation. Without doubt they fought too doggedly, clinging resolutely to the mere holding of ground, with the result that losses were heavy. The deep dug-outs and cellars often became fatal man traps. The use of the rifle was being forgotten, hand grenades had become the chief weapon, and the equipment of the infantry with machine guns and similar weapons had fallen far behind that of the enemy. The Field Marshal and I could for the moment only ask that the front lines should be held more lightly, the deep underground works be destroyed, and all trenches and posts be given up if the retention of them were unnecessary to the maintenance of the position as a whole, and likely to be the cause of heavy losses.

This was an extremely interesting statement, for though many commentators since 1918 have concentrated on trying to explain the new methods of tank and 'Stormtroop' breakthrough, it appears that there was another phenomenon afoot by the end of the war. This was that both sides had realised that in the face of overwhelming odds, mobility itself could be used as a form of protection. Not only had the ability to break fixed defences come on in leaps and bounds, but defenders comprehended that sometimes there could be utility in allowing the enemy to occupy the few kilometres of churned mud which was so difficult to cross and so difficult to fight in. Advances in both attack and defence therefore helped to end the trench war.

During much of the Great War, German casualties were persistently lower than those of the Entente powers that faced them. This disparity was probably at its greatest in the East. Nevertheless, it was also apparent in the West, where, for example, on the British sector of the Western Front, until the last two months of the war, nearly three British soldiers are thought to have fallen for every two German. The traditional explanation for this phenomenon is that the German Army had a higher level of 'military efficiency' than its enemies. This may have been true. It some places it certainly was, especially when the comparison was with the demonstrably underfed, under-armed, transport-starved, and sometimes poorly led Russians; but there is another equally good reason. This is that the German defensive positions did their work all too well. Detailed examination of the German and British losses shows that from February 1915 to December 1917 there were only two months when more Germans died than British. For almost all of this time the German Army stood on the defensive, and the greatest disparities occurred during some of the most significant British offensives. It is therefore apparent that on the Western Front one of the biggest factors saving German lives was being on the defence, and this defence was undoubtedly made all the more efficient both by tactics and fortifications.

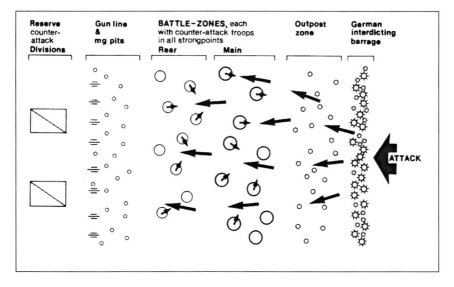

German 'web' defence, First World War, after the Battle of the Somme. Attacks are split up and canalized as they advance into the web, and are then counter-attacked. (Image courtesy of Paddy Griffith/Antony Bird Publications)

5

The 'Stormtroop' idea

As we have seen, three special *Versuchstruppen* were established by Colonel Max Bauer at the behest of the General Staff early in 1915. These experimental units were to test trench mortars, flame-throwers, and small 'assault cannon' respectively, their ultimate *raison d'être* being to spread the knowledge so gained throughout the army. The activity of these 'trailblazing' units might even lead eventually to the discovery of new methods to create gaps in enemy trench lines large enough for conventional units to pass through, thus leading to the resumption of the war of manoeuvre. Whilst the trench mortar- and flame-testing units were generally profitable, and did indeed lead to the adoption of new equipment and tactics, it is the *Sturmkanonen* unit commanded by Major Kalsow, founded by order of 2 March 1915, that has come to be regarded as the ancestor of all 'Stormtroop' units.

The degree to which there is a direct and necessary connection, or even a genuine lineage, is debatable, given the extent to which *Stoss* tactics were already beginning to catch on elsewhere, as for example in the general deployment of 'hand-grenade squads'. It should also be remembered that at least some other formations, such as the *Garde Schutzen Bataillon,* formed their own 'assault companies' at roughly the same time as the official experimental units, and probably independently of orders from the highest levels. Some of these were used as raiding parties, acting in formations of their own devising or as loose collections of individuals. Certainly, there was a degree of mythologising of the ancestry of the Stormtrooper, which was encouraged during the inter-war period by a variety of publications. These works included Bauer's own book *Der Grosse*

Krieg, a number of unit histories, a respected and much-copied encyclopaedia article by Major Berktau, and a PhD thesis by Gruss entitled *Aufbau und Verwendung der Deutschen Sturmbataillone in Weltkrieg* ('Establishment and Use of the German Storm Battalions in the World War'). Nevertheless, what the experimental troops did do was to bring together a range of disparate ideas and equipments, and, in the most valid and immediate way possible, subject them to the test of war. They were also the mechanism by means of which the General Staff generated a standard model and systematically analysed the results. To this extent at least, the history of Kalsow, Rohr, and their men is highly significant and bears repeating.

Kalsow's first task was to bring together a headquarters section, two companies of engineers and a detachment of twenty light-weight 3.7cm cannons recently developed by the firm Krupp. The troops came not from elite formations, but predominantly from *Ersatz*, or supplementary units. The next job was to practise attacks against dummy trench lines. During the spring of 1915 this work was carried out on artillery ranges well away from the front line near Cologne, but by May a practical set of tactics appeared to have been formulated. Following a traditional bombardment from covering artillery, the engineers would send parties forward protected by armoured shields to prepare the way for the little guns. The Krupp *Sturmkanonen* would then be pushed up, perhaps fifty to seventy-five metres apart, to engage any machine guns or nests of resistance left untouched by the preparatory shelling. Having neutralised enemy resistance, the remainder of the *Sturmabteilung* would come forwards, bombing and fighting their way through any remaining opposition.

Kalsow was committed to putting what was now known as the *Sturmabteilung* into action on the Western Front in June. The results were disappointing, and two factors seem to have frustrated what might otherwise have been a highly profitable experiment. The first was that a 3.7cm projectile was really too light to deal with trench fortifications, and though their effect was limited, the guns were betrayed by a large muzzle flash. The second reason for lack of success was that rather than holding the *Sturmabteilung* back in a rear area until the chance for a decisive blow manifested itself, Kalsow's men and guns were committed prematurely to the line. Losses were alarmingly high: of a unit only 649 strong, 184 men became casualties and six guns were lost in the first two weeks alone. These trained men proved difficult to replace quickly, with the result that *Sturmabteilung* Kalsow was out of action for some time.

Bauer's reaction was unforgiving, and in his memoirs he would describe the unfortunate Kalsow as 'an engineer who considered his troops as such'. On 8 September 1915 Kalsow was therefore replaced by *Hauptmann* Wilhelm Rohr, an aggressive and 'outstanding' 38-year-old officer. Rohr had previously served as a company commander with the *Garde Schutzen* and already had a record of innovative offensive action at the head of shock troops; moreover, he had new 'tactical and technical ideas'. Bauer was very clear from the outset that he regarded the formation as a '*Lehrtrupp*' (a 'learning' or 'teaching' unit), which would 'receive and test' new '*Kampfmittel*' (battle equipment). Rohr was certainly favoured from on high as his unit was described as the Crown Prince's '*Lieblingstruppe*', or favourite unit. A practical demonstration of this would be provided the following year when Hindenburg and Ludendorff visited the Western Front together. As Hindenburg recalled:

> On the way there … the German Crown Prince joined us and honoured me at Montmedy by parading a Storm company at the station. This reception was thoroughly in keeping with the chivalrous habit of mind of this exalted young Prince. His merry, frank manner and sound military judgement have always given me pleasure and confidence.

'Little Willy's' action also had the effect of parading Stormtroops in front of the top commanders who really mattered, and had the ultimate power to make productive use of them.

Fortune or good sense also smiled on Rohr in another way, for about the time of the arrival of the *Sturmabteilung* with General Gaede's forces at the end of the summer of 1915, its equipment was re-balanced and reinforced to incorporate a mixture of weapons. These included initially two, later six, machine guns (the equivalent of a full machine gun company); four light mortars; and six of the precious flame-throwers. The relatively ineffectual 3.7cm guns were later replaced with a full battery of mountain howitzers, which packed a far bigger punch. The unit now had the weaponry with which to tackle most tasks out of its own resources. The use of mortars and other supporting weapons as 'organic', or integral to the unit, as *Truppwaffen* was highly significant for it allowed the unit commander to quickly target local threats without long-winded or uncertain recourse to the artillery proper. Other units were already mixing machine guns on trench mounts, grenadiers and riflemen in new ways, but the *Sturmabteilung* was a quantum leap forward in that it mixed in an unfettered way what had previously been artillery and engineer resources. Part of the credit for this must go to Rohr and Reddemann, who seem to have co-operated in an exemplary manner; part to Max Bauer, who had the vision to make the experiments possible, and the political clout to protect the micro-tacticians from any untoward jealousy on the part of the established infantry, artillery and engineer hierarchies.

Sturmabteilung Rohr was first committed to action at the Schratzmannle on 12 October 1915, but rather than risk the whole unit, one company was used in concert with 187th infantry regiment. The attack began with the discharge of six large flame-throwers, following which small Stormtroop squads leapt into the newly cleared French trench and used grenades to quell anyone bold enough to challenge them. Intervention by enemy machine guns was countered by mortars and artillery specially deputed for the task. Ordinary infantrymen carrying the materials to block off the newly captured trench system now came over and consolidated the position firmly against any possible counterstroke. This, and other small actions during the winter, soon demonstrated the validity of the new tactics. As soon as December 1915 it is recorded that Rohr's unit began to fulfil its didactic function by hosting a six-day course for 400 members of 12th *Landwehr* Division – thus was spread the fruits of first experience.

Another of the early tasks of Rohr's men was the testing of the new *Stahlhelm*, or steel helmet. Bauer claimed that in fact he had realised as early as 1900 that 'the smallest shell splinter' was capable of penetrating both the leather *Pickelhaube* and skull behind it, and that he had raised the question of better head protection within the General Staff in 1912. Not until after the outbreak of war, however, and against a background of a rising toll of head injuries, was anything practical done about this matter. The very first helmet was a rather thick, heavy object: a skull piece on an orthopaedic-looking leather backing, with a Norman-style nasal guard. It was a local issue of 1,500 pieces only. These went to Army Group Gaede, and almost had to be paid for personally by Lieutenant Colonel Hesse, who seems to have procured them on his own initiative. Obviously, something much better was in order, and now official steps were put in train to provide a helmet which could be manufactured in quantity.

The impetus for what we now know as the German steel helmet appears to have come from Dr August Bier and Professor *Hauptmann* Friedrich Schwerd. The former provided statistical evidence as to the type of missiles causing head injury, and the latter set out to design the optimum shape and thickness of helmet to prevent the maximum number of these wounds. Experimental models were ready by 20 September 1915. Ballistic testing on Kummersdorf artillery range was carried out in November, and Rohr's men got some of the new headgear during December. On 14 December the War Ministry was able to announce that 30,000 of the helmets would be available in January 1916. Later, Rohr's battalion would also be called upon to test new models of body armour. These were not quite so successful, but did get issued on a limited scale.

It was also in January 1916 that *Sturmabteilung* Rohr fought one of its most famous actions, leading larger units of infantry in the successful attack on the Hartmannsweilerkopf. Doubtless, this was a particularly sweet moment for Rohr himself, as he had fought here before with the Guards. By February 1916 Rohr's detachment found itself part of Fifth Army at Verdun, where it was thrown into the maelstrom together with more conventional infantry formations and Guard Pioneers with their flame-throwers. Casualties now escalated, and the unit was withdrawn from the front to Doncourt after about three weeks, but the High Command was impressed enough to expand the experimental *Sturmabteilung* into a full-blown battalion. At the same time, many infantry regiments also deployed storm platoons or storm companies, for attacks on specific strong points in the French defences.

In May 1916 the High Command ordered that all the armies on the Western Front should send small cadres of officers and NCOs to the new *Sturmbataillon*. Thereafter, these personnel were to return to their own formations where they would train more units in the new tactics. Progress was uneven, owing to the pressures of active service, the difficulties of supplying enough new equipment, and the time taken to train the trainers, but soon dozens of new *Sturm* units were beginning to appear. So many were in fact formed during the latter part of 1916 that by November of that year a majority of divisions had at least one *Sturmabteilung* of about company strength, and some others had them as part of regimental strengths. A whole *Jäger*, or light infantry battalion, was also converted wholesale to create a new *Sturmbataillon*.

Even before this wave of training and conversion was complete, new orders were issued that every army was to have its own battalion-strength *Sturm* unit. More men were trained, and many of the extant company-sized units were brought together to form numbered battalions. Before the end of 1916 no less than sixteen *Sturm* battalions were in existence: ten in the west, five in the east and one with the Bulgarians. Usually, the identifying number of the battalion agreed with the number of the army to which it was attached. Some of the units had an Austro-Hungarian company allotted, and later, a further battalion was formed for the Italian front. As far as possible, the rank and file Stormtroopers were to be volunteers, young, unmarried, and physically fit. Unsurprisingly, quite a few men failed to come up to the mark and were returned to the units from which they came. Interestingly, Bauer seems to have regretted that the Stormtroop units were expanded as much as they were, for by adopting this course he believed they increasingly sacrificed their underlying principle. They were now set up – wrongly in his opinion – as *Elitestosstruppen*, 'elite shock troops', which was not what he had intended. Nevertheless, the idea of trying to train as much of the German army in the new tactics as was practicable continued. The Stormtroops were therefore both a useful reserve of quality assault troops, and what Ludendorff described as 'examples to be imitated by other men'. As *Major* Berktau put it so eloquently, the Stormtroops were *Lehrtruppe* and *Kampftruppe*, both teachers and battle troops for the hardest assignments.

The *Sturmbataillon* establishments varied in detail and over time, but at full strength numbered up to 1,400 men. These were divided into anything up to five *Sturmkompagnien*; first six, and later twelve, heavy machine guns in one or two companies; a battery of direct support infantry artillery; a mortar company with eight weapons; and a troop of about half a dozen flame-throwers. Berktau records the strength of the individual Storm companies as being five officers and 263 men; the machine gun company as four officers and 85 men; and the mortar company as two officers and 108 men. Where the infantry support artillery company was four modified 7.62cm guns, this element numbered three officers and 76 men. Rohr's own 5th Storm battalion was probably one of the strongest, boasting five *Sturm* companies, two machine gun, one artillery, and one mortar company. The *Sturmtruppe Picht*, which fought in Romania in late 1916, was put together using personnel from 148th infantry regiment, cavalry units, artillery and some men from a Bosnian unit in Austro-Hungarian service. This had four *Sturm* companies and a machine gun company, plus ancillary units.

Rohr and others had soon discovered that the full-length rifle was something of a handicap when involved in trench fighting and handling ancillary weapons, so shorter carbines of the sort already used by the Pioneers and cavalry were widely used by the Stormtroops. Whilst the artillery and pioneer elements of the *Sturmbataillon* were allowed to retain the distinctions of their arm of service on their uniforms, the ordinary infantry dress and equipment was modified to suit the special hard service, and dash, of the Stormtrooper. Thus it is that Berktau records the Storm battalion troops as being equipped with: 'Steel helmet, *Gebirgshosen*, [literally "mountain trousers"] with leather patches to buttocks and knees, mountain boots, puttees, entrenching tools, picks, and larger spades, hatchets, wire cutters, two *Feldflaschen* [water bottles] per man, carbine and bayonet. NCOs and communications troops were armed with semi automatic pistols'. As befitting the *Sturm* units' frequent use of hand grenades, the ordinary private soldiers were not designated as 'rifleman' or 'fusilier' but *Grenadiere* – Grenadiers. The significant exception to this rule was Rohr's own battalion, which retained pioneer titles and distinctions.

As we have seen, the strongest single motivating force behind the evolution of Stormtroop tactics was the need to find methods for breaking into, and through, trench lines. New *Stoss*, or shock, methods were already appearing in other units, for the same reason, even as Kalsow and Rohr did their work. Yet there were other needs, and sources of inspiration, which appear to have had a bearing on the development of German infantry assault tactics. It has been remarked, for example, that the methods and equipment of the mountain troops, or *Gebirgsjäger,* were a significant influence on both Stormtroops and the development of new tactics in general. Whilst German sources are generally inexplicit regarding the early links, there were certainly parallels, as for example in dress, and the necessity for mountain troops – frequently isolated in inhospitable terrain – to act on local initiative. *Major* Alfred Steinitzer's Bavarian *Schneeschuh Battalion Nr 1* was officially incorporated as early as November 1914, and it is interesting to note that at an early stage mountain companies incorporated both rifle and machine gun platoons – thus integrating different weapons at a lower level of organisation than was usual in the line infantry. Mountain terrain, which frequently forced advances through passes or along ski paths, was doubtless instrumental in causing tactical development in depth, and in encouraging the use of small groups, rather than endorsing the old linear patterns in which infantry were accustomed to fight.

In any event, units of mountain artillery and mortars were also formed, and by May 1915 the *Alpenkorps* was founded. Interestingly, this would be deployed not only in the high mountains of Italy and the Carpathians, but at Verdun, in Picardy, and in the Argonne, suggesting a general competence as assault troops as well as in their specialist role. As US intelligence observed at the end of the war, 'the Alpine Corps was considered one of the best German units'. The 200th Division, formed essentially of *Jäger* and ski-trained troops in 1916, was cast in the same mould. Whilst Bavarians bulked large in the *Gebirgsjäger,* the role of the Wurttembergers was not inconsiderable, and immortalised for posterity in the writings of Erwin Rommel. The Wurttemberg Mountain Battalion under Major Sprosser was raised at Munsingen in October 1915, and from the start included six companies and six mountain machine gun platoons. Interestingly, even their first deployment in the High Vosges was in terrain where it did not prove possible to man a continuous trench line but necessitated a series of strong points with 'all round defence'. Thereafter a good deal of the battalion's work in Italy and Romania involved both platoon-level actions and attacks in which the Wurttembergers were able to pass through enemy positions before attacking the flanks and rear areas. They thus had a general relevance to the formulation of 'infiltration' ideas. Whilst many of the battalion's later mountain battles took place in 1917 and were just one of several sources of inspiration for those compiling tactical doctrine in the last two years of the war, their impact on the later techniques of Rommel himself is indisputable.

Raids were similarly an important testing ground for unusual tactics. Gudmundsson has offered us two excellent examples of German raids that used innovative methods, and were illustrative of the improvements in minor tactics and the co-ordination of infantry with other arms. In July 1916 the 229th Reserve Infantry Regiment mounted the *Wilhelm* raid against the enemy south west of Lille. Intriguingly, the order to mount the attack, a single-page letter, stemmed from the commanding general of 50th Reserve Division, but did not specify an exact objective. Detailed planning was thus left to the regiment, which also co-ordinated the activities of supporting artillery and pioneer units. Four officers, twelve NCOs and 48 men formed the raiding force proper, with an additional group held in reserve. These personnel had previously been brought together to serve as an ad hoc regimental 'assault detachment', and were reassembled again for raiding missions. Questions of detail, including weapons and ammunition to be carried, were devolved to the detachment commander, *Leutnant* von Werner. The artillery component would include not only mortars but ten batteries of light and heavy artillery, first to prepare the ground, then form a 'box barrage' around the target area. Interestingly, the German raid coincided with the execution of a raid by New Zealanders nearby, and this nearly led to the abandonment of *Wilhelm*. The 229th carried on, hoping to take advantage of the confused situation, but found the defenders resolute and one portion of the attackers proved completely unable to enter the New Zealander's line. The Germans lost four dead, two missing and fourteen wounded, against which they captured two, killed one and wounded three of the opposition, whilst one New Zealander went missing.

In the *Jacobsbrunnen* raid of November 1917 the 7th Bavarian *Landwehr* were pitted against newly committed American troops in a quiet sector of Lorraine. This time there was even more artillery support, from no less than 17 batteries, and the raiders numbered well over 200 troops, drawn from not only the Bavarian *Landwehr* but other supporting elements including the divisional assault unit. Short salvoes of artillery fire covered the move forward in the darkness, and then the Pioneers broke through the obstacle zone with bangalore torpedoes. The raiders then broke into the enemy trenches, bombing and fighting their way along, killing a number of the Americans and capturing eleven in exchange for relatively modest losses of their own.

Yet these were but two of literally hundreds of missions mounted, and were in fact comparatively late essays in an art which was by now virtually perfected. Arguably, the developmental influence of raiding goes back much further. In many instances there was little to distinguish early 'raids' from rather more innocuous-sounding 'patrols', and both had begun before the end of 1914. Quite a few of the first missions were relatively crude affairs, and were often on a tiny scale, mounted for limited objectives, perhaps to be a 'nuisance' to an already jittery enemy, or to determine his strength and dispositions. One British Tommy later spoke of the fear, early in the war, of German bogeymen, on the loose late at night, with massive 'truncheons' (trench clubs) who would attempt to strike at a victim's head before pulling him bodily from the trench. In the roughest sense, such ventures were certainly experimental. Just one of these diminutive and potentially deadly nocturnal scuffles was mounted by a small group drawn from 36th Fusilier Regiment against the French, in the summer of 1915, and was later recorded first hand by its *Leutnant* commander:

It rained in torrents the whole night. Better patrol weather one couldn't have hoped for. At three in the morning I was roused by the *Unteroffizer* of the watch. At 3.30 we were underway. Everything had been prepared the day before. Each of us had seen the terrain through the binoculars. We were seven altogether, myself, a *Vizfeldwebel*, an *Unteroffizier*, and four men. We wanted to penetrate a sap by daybreak, cutting off a post, or at least to ascertain the number of the regiment dug in opposite. At exactly 3.30 we left our trenches. Every man had already checked his pistol and hand grenades … Pitch black. 300 metres to go to the sap. Carefully traversing our own entanglement we listened for a moment – on the other side everything is quiet, no rifle shot, only now and then, further off, the odd Very pistol flare. The Frenchmen suspected nothing, as we came on such a foul night, although our frequent patrols should have made them vigilant. So step by step forwards. Fusilier 'F' and me to the front, left and right a man as protection, the rest tightly behind. Feeling the way from shell hole to shell hole, through great bomb craters and climbing over trees felled by gun fire, trying anxiously to avoid any crack from the wood underfoot. Now and then we lie down for a moment and strain our ears. Suddenly, to our right front, a flare goes up. We lie fixed to the spot. Are we noticed? – Everything stays quiet. The rain continues unabated. Our luck. 4.45 finds us by the sap. It becomes gradually lighter. With one of the men I crept cautiously closer. Nothing stirred. The sap is unoccupied. But why did no one come to the sap? After the discovery of our last patrol the French had built a wall of 'Spanish Riders' [wooden obstacles with spikes] and barbed wire across the sap. With our single pair of wire cutters we could not do much. But we didn't want to have got soaked for nothing …

So it was, by whispers and signs, the seven raiders deployed in ambush, clutching their pistols and daggers. Before long, steps were heard and an enemy officer in kepi and grey raincoat came walking down the trench. The German officer jumped down into the trench to seize the unfortunate by the throat and press his dagger to his chest, but the enemy struggled, grappling with him in the wet. Another German attempted to secure him, but in the fracas both headgear and dagger fell into the mud on the floor of the trench, and shrieks from the French officer drew his men running:

Then clearly I saw on the coat collar the number 102, white on black. Already some Frenchmen had arrived; the first without a helmet, half dressed, shoots without taking aim … with all my strength I punched my Frenchman in the face and he lets me go.

So ended this 'raid' with the Fusiliers scrambling back into the darkness, with two pieces of information: that the sap was blocked, and the French regiment was the 102nd.

To be valuable learning tools for new minor tactical methods, the gleanings of raids had to be examined, distilled, and circulated. Probably one raid more than any other fulfilled this purpose, and, remarkably, documentation of its planning, execution and results was not only prepared for German eyes, but promptly fell into Allied hands, so that within four months the enemy too had learned many of its lessons. This raid was the attack of 11 April 1916 on 'the *Spion*' near La Boiselle, mounted by a fifty-man detachment of 110th Reserve Infantry Regiment and four Pioneers, the attackers being commanded by *Hauptmann* Wagener. Of these, roughly two-thirds were to climb from the *Blaue Stellung* to creep up on the enemy, whilst the remainder formed a support group. The key to the success of the mission was to be a diversionary attack and the close co-operation of machine guns and artillery, as the planning document, written by Wagener himself, explained:

> For 25 minutes before the commencement of the raid the artillery will prepare for the assault by shelling the enemy's trenches between *Besenhecke* and the *Windmühle*, and also the *Weisse Steinmauer*. During the raid the artillery will control by its fire all the enemy's trenches likely to be a source of danger to the enterprise. In order to draw the fire of the enemy's artillery away from the spot to be raided a feint attack against the enemy's position just north of la Boiselle Cemetery will start 15 minutes before the artillery opens fire. In order that the registration of the objective by the heavy artillery and Minenwerfer shall not be apparent, on the morning of the day before the raid ... a feint bombardment of target sectors 76 to 79 will be carried out, combined with a mine explosion, with the object of misleading the enemy ... The machine gun officer will arrange that, during the whole time of the raid the enemy's rear trenches in target sectors 76 to 81 are kept under a constant fire, with a view to causing him all possible loss.

Further mortar and artillery work included extensive wire cutting, and a heavy *Albrecht* mortar firing into the enemy trenches nearby.

The raiders themselves were to go 'in attack order without great-coat or cap, belts to be worn without pouches, gas masks to be slung and tucked into the tunic'. Of those to penetrate the enemy defences, half would be armed with pistols, half with rifles. Those 'supporting' would mainly carry rifles, and all parties would take grenades. Perhaps fearful of suffering friendly fire, Wagener's team would all be identified by a 'triangle of white linen sewn on the breast and back'. Their key objective was to take as many prisoners as possible, and as many rifles, machine guns, packs etc. as could be carried back. On the command of *Leutnant* Stradtmann, or the 'charge' signal by a bugler kept by the Captain for the purpose, the raiding party was to retire to the dugout from which they started. Prudently, Wagener called upon Assistant Surgeon Wisser to set up a dressing station near the jumping-off point.

Despite adverse circumstances, including spirited resistance and wafting gas that caused problems for the attackers, the raid was a huge success. Following the bombardments and distractions *Leutnant* Stradtmann's party was first into the British trenches and swiftly secured three prisoners. Joined by the others they then overcame a small group of the enemy, even though they were armed with 'hand grenades and rifles with bayonets fixed'. Next they encountered a damaged machine gun emplacement where Reservist Nadolny attempted to dig out the weapon. Meanwhile, a few more enemy troops come up a communication trench, but were bayoneted by three Germans. Further along the trench, dead enemies were found in a dugout, but Dumas's patrol was set upon by British troops who engaged them in a melee with rifles, grenades and pistols, but the enemy were seen off or captured. As a fight appeared to be developing on the left, a few reinforcements and the regimental adjutant, wearing full breathing apparatus, entered the fray. On the right, Freund's patrol did well, capturing some more of the British and bayoneting others: 'A few Englishmen attempted to get away, but were shot dead'. Others ran into the box barrage around the target sector, and were forced pell mell back into the raiders. The entire party was back in the German lines within approximately twenty minutes of leaving it. The final tally of enemy captured included 24 fit and five wounded 'Englishmen' mainly of the Royal Irish Rifles, and a selection of equipment. Many others were obviously killed, whilst the Germans had a few minor wounds, the worst of which was a man cut across the forehead with a grenade fragment who was immediately able to rejoin his unit after treatment.

The action formed the basis of no less than three reports at various levels. A number of significant conclusions were drawn, including the value of gas as a discomfort and distraction, though the difficulty, if not impossibility, of conducting a complete raid in gas masks was noted. Prior shelling was also seen as extremely useful, not because it had any chance of annihilating the enemy, but because it tended to cause the enemy to spread out into 'isolated groups' whose morale would suffer further if any of their number were killed or injured. In the case of the *Spion* raid it was noted that the supporting batteries and mortars fired about 6,000 rounds, ranging from small field-gun rounds right up to 21cm shells. Whilst reports of the planning and action made a useful template for further raids, widening distribution did nothing for secrecy. Wagener himself appears to have distributed forty copies of one of his reports, and within a few weeks the British had not only Wagener's words translated but a copy of the fire plan and 'deductions' drawn – virtually everything was being studied on the other side of the line by August 1916. Arguably, both sides had learned from this model raid, and the German perpetrators had gained, at best, four months' headway in digesting the lessons. It was also true that the Canadians were already using many similar methods, and information regarding these had already been circulated to British and other Empire formations prior to this date. As in so many fields, the tactical advance was incremental, and learning from the opposition was crucial.

It cannot be doubted that the very notion of the Stormtrooper had a propaganda value: a power to raise uncertainty in the hearts of the enemy, and give a fillip to those fighting by their sides. The celebrity of the few could, however, be a double-edged weapon, as was recorded by German Medical Officer Stefan Westmann:

> The men of the storm battalions were treated like football stars. They lived in comfortable quarters, they travelled to the 'playing ground' in buses, they did their jobs and disappeared again, and left the poor

foot sloggers to dig in, to deal with the counter-attacks and endure the avenging artillery fire of the enemy. They were so well trained and had developed such a high standard of team work ... They moved like snakes over the ground, camouflaged and making use of every bit of cover, so that they did not offer any targets for artillery fire.

It has been said that Stormtroop units suffered disproportionately high casualties, due to the difficulty of the tasks they were given and the single-minded determination with which they were carried out. Conversely, it has been suggested that Stormtroop units actually suffered lower casualties because of their new tactics, and because they were specially chosen as fit men who were withdrawn between operations. Curiously, both of these statements may be correct, with heavy casualties for limited periods being balanced out by periods of training. The statistical information as available at this time appears inconclusive. Rohr's battalion, numbered 5th 'Royal Prussian' *Sturmbataillon*, after it was attached to 5th Army, is known to have suffered 621 fatalities during the period of its existence. Not all dates of death are known, but 74 died in 1915, 156 in 1916, 118 in 1917, and 1918 was easily the worst year, with 187 or more fatalities. The most senior member to die was *Hauptmann* Siegfried Hoffmann of the first *Sturmkompagnie*, on 30 March 1918, one of twenty officers killed or who had died with the battalion. Interestingly, eight of Rohr's command died in accidents, and of these, six (roughly one per cent of all fatalities) happened on the *Übungsplatz*, or training ground. This and the fact that one of these, *Leutnant* Heinrich Hermanns, was even an officer, speak volumes about rigorous training and the use of live munitions.

Given that different units had very different service, exact comparisons are difficult, but we do know that many German infantry battalions suffered more than a thousand fatalities during the war. The *Colbergsches Grenadier-Regiment Nr 9*, for example, lost 454 officers and 4660 men, which suggests that each of its three battalions had in excess of 1200 fatalities. Two Majors were killed with the regiment. The Bremen infantry regiment *Nr 75*, similarly, had over 1000 dead per battalion, and this was probably not untypical. On the other side of the line, 2nd Battalion of the Manchesters, with long service on the Western Front, had a comparable 1,165 war dead. Perhaps surprisingly, 11th Battalion of the East Lancashire Regiment (or 'Accrington Pals'), a unit often held up as particularly inexperienced, and which was 'slaughtered' on the first day of the Somme, had 729 killed or missing over the duration of the war, of whom 24 were officers. Moreover, some of the 'missing' turned up in German prisoner of war camps, and one or two, including one officer, actually died in German captivity.

Another stereotype that may require challenging is that after the initial raising of the first *Sturmbataillon*, all storm or shock troops were young, fit men. Again, the figures we have are no more than fragmentary, but what we do know shows that, even if this was generally true, there were definite exceptions to the rule. *Sturmtruppe Picht* fighting in Romania in late October and early November 1916 suffered 95 casualties, of all descriptions, including 'lightly wounded'. Of these 95 men, no less than 44% were aged over 25, and 15% were over 30. In *Sturmkompanie* 4 a number of men were certainly veterans, to put it kindly. *Landsturm* other rank Adolf Ruhr was almost 41 when he got hit; *Feldwebel* Waldemar Verch had the bad luck to be wounded on his 40th birthday. Another man, Albert Broze, was 39. It is also worth observing that, generally speaking, 'veteran' troops were less likely to get hurt than callow novices, so the likelihood is that rather than being the older members of the unit, the casualties were, on average, younger.

It is also the case that the efforts of the Stormtroop battalions as innovators and trainers were not carried out in isolation. Training in specialist weapons continued elsewhere, as did officer schools, whose syllabuses stressed leading under the new conditions of war. It also needs to be remembered that the Prussian Guard had a *Lehr*, or instructional, unit even before the start of the war. Intensive retraining of company and battalion commanders was commenced in October 1916, and 'leadership' courses for more senior officers were established within both the Army Groups of Prince Rupprecht and the Crown Prince. In the winter of 1917 to 1918 there was finally an opportunity to give huge bodies of men additional training in new tactical methods, as the Russians collapsed and divisions were transferred to the West. This massive effort was a partial success as the early breakthroughs would demonstrate, and personal accounts from some divisions show a very thorough training regime. The 1st Bavarian Division, for example, spent January 1918 training in the Champagne. Next they moved on to Eighteenth Army at Vervins where they were taught or refreshed on discipline, advancing, terrain skills and machine guns. After this there were exercises which included such advanced matters as working with other divisions, and manoeuvre with tanks and aircraft.

This was model practice, but very far from all the German army would be 'Stormtroop trained' and able for offensive action. Large numbers of men were too old to be really fit, some of the *Landsturm* for example being over fifty, and some new recruits had merely grasped the rudiments. Some otherwise useful men were debilitated by wounds or gas. Supplies of new equipment were not inexhaustible. The result was a grading of different divisions as to their suitability for offensive action, and whilst some were *Angriff* ('attack', or 'assault'), others were merely *Stellungs,* troops capable of holding a position. At best, the work of the 'recruit depots' just behind the line and that of the Storm battalions was incomplete. Having spent part of 1917 in training other troops, notably infantry gun battery crews, Rohr's own battalion was itself recommitted to the fray in the great offensives of early 1918. It fought first as two half battalions, and later as a single unit, before returning to training again and working with both the Guard cavalry and Austrian units. Finally, and perhaps fittingly, the last duty of *Sturmbataillone* Rohr was to act as the Army Headquarters Guard unit, probably being regarded by now as the most reliable battalion in the German army.

6

Machine Gun Tactics

Machine gun tactics developed from a base of almost nothing prior to 1900 to a situation in 1914 where the relatively small numbers of weapons available were often capable of an extreme and disproportionate influence in battle. As trench garrisons were thinned out and attacking formations were likewise made less dense and linear, machine guns continued to increase their importance. This was not to say that they were the prime killers of trench warfare – this dubious distinction fell to the artillery – nor that machine guns were equally useful in all circumstances. For whilst, as we have seen, machine guns were pushed well forward into German attacks on trench lines early in the war, for a long time they remained most potent in defence. This was partly a question of the evolution of suitable offensive tactics, but it was also a natural function of the attributes of the standard 'Model 08' machine gun, which was heavy, water-cooled, and fired from 250-round cloth belts. The gun itself weighed 22kg, whilst the standard *Schlitten* or 'sledge' mount, a thoroughly stable adjustable platform, added a further 34kg. At least one propaganda picture showed a German soldier carrying the whole paraphernalia, mounted barrel and all, on his broad shoulders, but this was a work of Hercules. The *Schlitten* was designed with handles for relatively easy carriage by two men, stretcher style, at waist or shoulder height, and when the going got tough on longer distances four men could take a handle each. In the deepest mud the load could be broken down even more, dismounting the gun barrel and hauling this between another two men. Broad leather 'dragging straps' helped a little when the load became irksome, hot, or freezing cold.

By itself, however, the gun was useless, and a single filled ammunition belt weighed in at 7kg. Little surprise then that for road transport the guns were either on limbered horse-drawn wagons, or hauled in little hand carts. Since a belt was enough for only a minute or less at rapid fire, or perhaps a maximum of four minutes at the slowest rate of ammunition conservation, many metal boxes of ammunition were needed. The usual allotment on hand for each gun in a six-gun company was 12,000 rounds, or forty-eight belts for each gun – a heap of boxes and cartridges weighing in excess of 2000kg for the group. During a battle the whole lot might be shot away very easily, leaving exhausted gunners and supply troops to replenish the stock from ammunition columns to the rear. On a really bad day this process might have to be repeated more than once, by which time it was likely that casualties would have been incurred. Additional inconveniences included the provision of spare parts, and water to cool the barrel jackets, plus a seventh gun held in reserve in case of emergency or catastrophic failure. For defensive work there were also armoured barrel jackets and gun shields. The heaviest of these weighed about 27kg, but protection had to be balanced against the additional weight. In the event, many guns in the West were used without the large crew shield, but often armoured barrel jackets and abbreviated muzzle shields were retained. For highly accurate long-range work – anything up to 2000 metres – another common piece of kit was the *Zielfernrohr* 12 optic sight. Interestingly, the actual battle range of the heavy machine gun was limited far more by visibility, terrain, weather, presence of cover, and skill of the gun crew than by the range of the bullet, which was anything up to a theoretical maximum of 4000 metres. The manual *Feld-Pioneer Dienst aller Waffen* of 1911 illustrated basic designs for open-topped machine gun pits which were roughly the shape of a truncated letter 'T' with its base toward the enemy. These could be deep to accommodate standing gunners, or relatively shallow for a seated firer; they might either be dug straight into the ground, or could make use of sandbags. All these designs and variations were replicated on the battlefields of 1914.

The importance placed on machine guns was marked by huge efforts to put more of such weapons in the hands of the troops. Supplementary units were soon raised, and with production of

MG 08 machine guns steadily increasing, a second machine gun company was added to regiments as soon as adequate numbers of weapons and trained men became available. Special 'Marksman' machine gun units were also raised and deployed to points on the front where there was particular need of their services. Almost 5,000 machine guns had been in the hands of the German army at the outbreak of war, but by 1916 a further 10,000 guns had been produced by the plant at Spandau, with several thousand more now coming from the DWM Berlin factory. Thereafter, production figures would rise ever more steeply until the total numbers of MG 08 guns made by November 1918 reached about 72,000 – roughly two thirds from DWM and the remainder from Spandau.

By 1916 experience had advanced to the point where fresh directives on the use of the MG 08 in trench warfare could be issued. One of the most important of these was the document *Regulations for Machine Gun Officers and Non Commissioned Officers*. This paper made clear that effective concealment was highly important: emplacements were to be so constructed as to avoid telltale heaps of earth as well as to 'cover the whole of the proscribed field of fire'. Usually, there would be two alternative positions nearby having much the same field of fire. No less than sixteen full boxes of ammunition were to be kept by the gun (4000 rounds), and when a box was expended it was to be replaced immediately from the belt store. During the day the machine gun was to be kept in a dugout, but by the steps ready to move; at night it would stand loaded and ready to fire in its emplacement. Three spare barrels were also to be kept near each gun, as was plenty of water in buckets and a butt for each gun. Protection of the gun and crew were critical, and for close defence six hand grenades were to be kept nearby. One armed sentry was to be posted by day, two by night, each having the use of a periscope.

In the event of 'sighting a particularly favourable target' or a surprise attack, the gun was to open fire immediately. Usually, the crew would check if friendly troops were out to the front before commencing fire, but this nicety would be dispensed with if the enemy attacked, not firing being more dangerous than the obvious risk to one's own men. Where possible, an immediate situation report was to be made to both the platoon commander and the sector machine gun officer. To make rapid and accurate firing possible, likely targets within the zone would be registered, and a range card made for easy adjustment of fire. 'Daily fire' could also be organised by the company commander, indicating in advance the targets to be engaged and the number of rounds to be fired.

Machine guns were relied upon more and more as a cornerstone of the defensive battle alongside artillery, rifles and grenades. The crucial thing was that they should be able to survive artillery bombardment, preferably in dugouts, and then be quickly deployed to firing positions on the surface. As eye witness Matthaus Gerster would record of the first day on the Somme, in *Die Schwaben an der Ancre* (The Schwabians on the Ancre):

> Looking towards the British trenches through the long trench periscopes held up out of the dugout entrances there could be seen a mass of steel helmets above the parapet showing that the storm troops were ready for the assault. At 7.30 am the hurricane of shells ceased as suddenly as it had begun. Our men at once clambered up the steep shafts leading from the dugouts to daylight and ran singly or in groups to the nearest shell craters. The machine guns were pulled out of the dugouts and hurriedly placed in position, their crews dragging the heavy ammunition boxes up the steps and out to the guns. A rough firing line was thus rapidly established. As soon as the men were in position, a series of extended lines of infantry were seen moving forward from the British trenches. The first line appeared to continue without without end to right and left. It was quickly followed by a second, then a third and fourth. They came on at a steady easy pace as if expecting to find nothing alive in our front trenches ... The front line, preceded by a thin line of skirmishers and bombers, was now half way across No Man's Land. 'Get ready' was passed along our front line from crater to crater, and heads appeared over the crater edges as final positions were taken up for the best view, and machine guns mounted firmly in place. A few minutes later, when the leading British line was within a hundred yards, the rattle of machine gun and rifle broke out along the whole line of shell holes. Some fired kneeling so as to get a better target over the broken ground, whilst others, in the excitement of the moment, stood up regardless of their own safety, to fire into the crowd of men in front

of them. Red rockets sped up into the blue sky as a signal to the artillery, and immediately afterwards a mass of shells from the German batteries in rear tore through the air and burst among the advancing lines. Whole sections seemed to fall, and the rear formations moving in close order, quickly scattered. The advance rapidly crumbled under this hail of shells and bullets. All along the line men could be seen throwing up their arms and collapsing, never to move again. Badly wounded rolled about in their agony, and others, less severely injured, crawled to the nearest shell hole for shelter … the extended lines, though badly shaken and with many gaps, now came on all the faster. Instead of a leisurely walk they covered the ground in short rushes at the double. Within a few minutes the leading troops had advanced within a stone's throw of our front trench, and while some of us continued to fire at point blank range, others threw hand grenades among them. The British bombers answered back, whilst the infantry rushed forward with fixed bayonets. The noise of the battle became indescribable. The shouting of orders and the shrill cheers as the British charged forward could be heard above the violent and intense fusillade of machine guns and rifles and bursting bombs, and above the deep thunderings of the artillery and shell explosions.

As orders of 6th Bavarian Division observed, the Somme showed the 'decisive value' of machine guns in defence, and the more the enemy bombarded the German trenches before attacking, 'the greater the extent to which we must rely on the employment of machine guns.' However, machine guns would only frustrate an attack if they could be kept in serviceable condition, and then 'brought up into the firing position in time'. This could now only be achieved if the majority of the machine guns was kept out of the front two lines trenches, as otherwise there was no certainty that the enemy's assault would be seen in time. Locating the emplacements behind the second, or even the third, line of trenches also put them in places where they were considerably less effected by methodical barrages. The individual fire positions were to be such that they flanked the trench systems, or provided wide fields of fire. A proportion of weapons were best kept well behind the trenches altogether, in covered deep pits, platforms in trees, hedges, or even out in the open provided the enemy could not register them before making an advance.

It was well appreciated that the great weight of a machine gun and its ammunition was a serious impediment, making it difficult to get the pieces out of secure dugouts and hiding places and quickly into firing positions. Accordingly, there were experiments with, and production of, expedient 'trench mounts' during 1915. These were in widespread use by 1916. They might incorporate a pivot on a wooden board, or a small, pronged stand which could achieve some stability when pressed into the soil. They were not, however, more than a temporary answer, and not calculated to produce very accurate fire. Moreover, since the gun barrel and jacket were retained along with the trailing belt, neither were they a completely effective solution to the weight problem.

Though German machine guns were rightly feared, in one vital aspect the development of German weapons and tactics lagged well behind what the British had pioneered as early as the end of 1914: the true 'light' machine gun. The American-designed Lewis gun, at first designated as an 'automatic rifle' had been tested even before the outbreak of war. By November 1914 an experimental handful had made their way to the front, being seen initially as stop-gap supplements to the inadequate numbers of 'heavy', tripod-mounted Vickers and Maxim guns on hand. Yet it was quickly realised that a lighter version of the machine gun that was air cooled and had a magazine attached rather than using trailing belts, offered far greater tactical flexibility. It could be carried by one man, set up in seconds, and work its way into positions otherwise impractical with large tripods and water canisters. Whilst in simple terms its raw firepower, range and accuracy were all inferior to the MG 08 or Vickers – points all amply noted by contemporaries – it opened up new possibilities for infantry tactics and organisation that were scarcely dreamed of prior to the war. Initially, both 'heavy' and 'light' machine guns coexisted within the British infantry battalions, but by 1916, with large numbers of Lewis guns now issued to the infantry, heavier weapons were withdrawn and grouped into companies and battalions of the new Machine Gun Corps. Within an infantry platoon a light machine gun could now operate as a mobile firebase, and a variety of tactics using grenades, rifles, bayonets and rifle grenades as a complementary group of weapons with different characteristics could begin to develop.

Many German commanders would have liked to have tried similar things at an early stage, but for most it was not to be. So it was
that whilst the Battle of the Somme inflicted massive casualties on
the attackers, the impact of the light machine gun was noted with
considerable trepidation and envy by German commanders. As
General von Stein, commander of XIV Reserve Corps, in charge of
the front between Monchy and the Somme reported to First Army
headquarters:

> The attack on the 1st July was well prepared, and the [British]
> infantry was splendidly equipped with all kinds of weapons for
> close combat. It was provided with large numbers of Lewis guns
> which were brought into action very quickly and skilfully in newly
> captured positions. It is very desirable that our infantry should be
> equipped with a large number of light machine guns of this descrip-
> tion in order to increase the intensity of its fire.

A few months later German IV Corps was commenting on the
way that British infantry had learned much since the autumn of
1915, specifically that 'The English infantry showed great tenacity in
defence. This was especially noticeable in the case of small parties,
which, once established with machine guns in the corner of a wood
or a group of houses, were very difficult to drive out'. One way to
counter these developments would be to increase the numbers of
German guns, preferably to thirty or more per regiment. Tactically,
it might then be possible to secure thinly held lines by 'placing supports (infantry and machine guns) distributed in groups according
to the ground, as close as possible behind the foremost front line'.
As regards specific designs of guns and mounts, the following sug-
gestion was made:

> Machine guns usually have to be brought up over open ground
> under a heavy barrage. The great weight of the gun has again proved
> to be a serious disadvantage under these conditions. Even if the
> gun is dismounted, it is very difficult to drag up the heavy sledge
> over ground which is under fire. All regiments are unanimous in
> recommending the introduction of a lighter form of gun carriage,
> modelled on that of the improvised gun carriage used by machine gun

marksman sections. One regiment has obtained good results with a gun carriage of its own invention, which is even lighter.

Design and production problems ensured that no quick answer was forthcoming. A few light machine guns had been obtained relatively quickly, and these were predominantly of three types: the Danish-designed Madsen, the home-grown Bergmann and some captured Lewis guns. The small numbers and disparate models used did not help, nor were the early tactics devised particularly advanced. The few Madsen-equipped *Musketen* units, for example, are recorded as being used essentially in a 'back stop' defensive role during the Battle of the Somme – the four-man gun teams being deployed just behind the front line to cover vulnerable gaps.

The ideal answer would have been a home-designed and produced true light machine gun that took the Lewis and other Allied and Central Powers weapons as a starting point and improved upon them in such a way as to make a highly portable arm to supplement the long-range heavy machine guns. This did not happen for a number of reasons. For one thing there was a fear that a truly new and effective design would take too long to produce, for another there were worries that it was difficult enough to train sufficient men on one type of gun without introducing something radical and untried in the midst of war. Therefore, the gun which was produced played safe, but still took time to get into the hands of the troops. The MG 08/15, as its name suggests, was first conceived in 1915, and was essentially a lighter variant of the old heavy MG 08. It retained the basic Maxim mechanism and a slightly smaller water jacket, but added a shoulder stock and small bipod. The whole outfit was still 20kg with the water jacket filled – or almost fifty per cent heavier than the Lewis gun.

Though eventually produced in large numbers by seven manufacturers, the MG 08/15 reached the troops only gradually. About 2,000 were made by the end of 1916, less than 50,000 during 1917, and the vast majority (over 80,000) were made during the last year of war. This cannot but have hindered the development of small-unit tactics, since the British, by comparison, had enough Lewis guns to begin the evolution of platoon action based around light machine guns as early as 1916. The total number of Lewis guns may eventually have been roughly the same as the total number of MG 08/15s produced, but British production was running roughly a calendar year ahead of German, with 25,000 made before 1916 was out. Elementary distinctions between the tactical roles of 'heavy' and 'light' machine guns were determined by the British early in 1916, with the manual *The Tactical Employment of Machine Guns and Lewis Guns* appearing in March. The widespread adoption of 'Lewis gun sections' within platoons in 1917 was formalised by February of that year with the *Instructions for the Training of Platoons for Offensive Action*.

Ludendorff was clearly frustrated by the slow tactical progress made with German light machine guns, as he later explained in his memoirs:

> In the infantry company the light machine gun had to become accepted as a normal part of the unit. It was still viewed as a weapon ancillary to the infantry. The fact that the light MG is itself part of the infantry and the infantry carry the gun had not yet penetrated into the marrow of the infantry, never mind the army. The light MG, because of its firepower, was and had to become the main component of the infantry's firepower in combat … Light machine gun and gun carrier formed groups of infantry marksmen who, if danger arose, if the fighting was a matter of life and death, had to hold together …

This statement was, however, at least slightly disingenuous for two reasons. Firstly, the infantry had very few light machine guns except what they could capture from the enemy until early 1917. It was not, therefore, reasonable to assume that they would absorb every tactical nuance as quickly as troops that had been armed with similar, or better, weapons for many months. Secondly, as First Quarter Master and most senior figure next to Hindenburg, it can reasonably be suggested that deficiencies in this department were at least partly Ludendorff's own responsibility.

So it was that although German light machine gun experiments and theory, as developed through the Stormtroops and other small units, may have been almost as well advanced as the enemy, practical implementation ran far behind and was made worse by the fact that the German front was inevitably much longer than that covered

by the British. The result was that at first there were only two MG
08/15s per infantry company, with a goal of three set for February
1917. Initially, these were pooled together within the fourth platoon
of the company. By the end of 1917 some companies on the Western
Front could boast as many as six light machine guns, but in the East
one or two remained the norm long afterwards. Only in January
1918 were there enough light machine guns to have a minimum of
four per company, making it possible to fully equip the assault units
deployed in the Spring Offensive. Now each platoon could have at
least one light machine gun squad of eight men, with four gunners
and ammunition carriers and four riflemen supporting them. This
allowed infantry tactics universally based upon platoons made up
of different types of *Gruppe* or squad, with each platoon having
the fully effective integral fire support of a machine gun. In some
instances, where there were enough machine weapons, a *Gruppe*
even operated as a mix, having a four-man machine gun section
combined with a larger number of riflemen. These fully integrated
squads were known as *Einheitsgruppen*, being 'uniform', 'single' or
'standard' squads.

   During 1918 the different types of squad were put together in
various proportions to create platoons with the flexibility required
for the task in hand. A good example of how this was achieved is
furnished by the elite Bavarian *Leib Regiment*. In its *Kampfzugen*,
or 'battle platoons', there were two *Einheitsgruppen* and an assault
squad or *Stossgruppe*. In the ordinary or 'line' platoons there were
four squads: two light machine gun, and two rifle. There were also
'expansion' platoons consisting essentially of a reserve of men, and
specialist squads for the grenade launcher and reconnaissance.
After the war, as the army was boiled down to its irreducible minimum, there would be greater uniformity and a generalised use of
the mixed *Einheitsgruppen* as genuinely standard units. So it is that
Bodo Zimmermann's inter-war manual *Die Soldatenfibel* shows
fourteen-man *Gruppe* comprising two *Truppe*, or sub section 'troops',
one being the *LMG Trupp* of four men, the other the *Schutzentrupp*,
or rifle troop of nine, the whole being led by a *Gruppenfuhrer*, or
squad leader.

   The clear distinction now drawn between the roles of the 'heavy'
and the 'light' machine guns was well illustrated by the 'Machine

Gunner's Catechism' captured from a prisoner of the 2nd Machine Gun Company of the 13th Wesphalian infantry regiment, by the French early in 1918. This simple 'question and answer' style document was apparently intended as a simple *aide-mémoire* of tactical battle tips for troops. According to this, the purpose of the 'heavy' MG 08 was to be the weapon of the *Zwischenfeld*, literally the 'midfield' or intermediate zone. Set up in reserve positions, supporting points and machine gun nests, and provided with dugouts and camouflage, its job was to act as a stop against any enemy penetrating through the first line so as to threaten German artillery. Given alternative positions, and guarded by a sentry to prevent it being taken by surprise, it was best located for flanking fire. It could similarly be used over obstacles, and against aircraft and tanks. It could also shoot over advancing friendly infantry, provided that there was at least five metres of overhead clearance.

For particular fire missions, heavy machine gun special tasks might include harassing fire and barrage fire. In the harassing role during daylight, it could be aimed 'upon the most frequented routes', and single shots used to discomfit anyone attempting movement. The weapon might also then be locked into position to cover the roads with bursts of fire at opportune moments. Barrages fired by groups of guns could be shot at long range to saturate particular target areas. Again, the objective might be as much to deny an area to the enemy as to destroy a designated target. By contrast, the 'light' machine gun was seen only as a front-line piece, to be 'par excellence … a weapon of defence against assault in the infantry lines'. Its usual position was loaded ready to fire in a dugout. From here it could also be carried forward into the attack. The first duty of its 'No 1' crewman, having reached the enemy trench was to 'make sure of a good field of fire, so as to be able to annihilate the enemy with his fire when the counter-attack is made'. Unlike its heavier cousin, the light machine gun was to limit its shooting to 'well-placed and visible' targets.

Useful as the MG 08/15 proved to be in finally liberating squads to act under their own covering fire, German commanders, including Ludendorff, were aware that it was not as light or handy as comparable US or British weapons. To this end, a new 'light' machine gun was under development at the end of hostilities. This was the Erfurt-made 08/18 which married up the familiar Maxim mechanism with a lighter air-cooled barrel. The new gun reached production stage, but it is unclear what, if any, combat they saw before the war ended.

7

Close Combat and the Tank

By the middle of the war the concept of *Stosskraft* ('shock' or 'impact' tactics) as distinct from *Feuerkraft*, or 'fire power', was well established. For the ordinary infantryman, competence in *Stosskraft* was gained essentially through familiarity and training with the weapons of close combat, or *Nahkampfmittel*. A short pamphlet of this title was issued under the auspices of the Chief of the German General Staff in August 1916, and thus must have been initially developed during the tenure of Falkenhayn, even though it is generally associated with the period in which Hindenburg held the highest military appointment and Ludendorff served as First Quartermaster-General. A second, and fuller, edition appeared on 1 January 1917. As might be expected, the grenade was given considerable prominence:

> For close combat, hand grenades are in every way as important as rifles and pistols. Every man of the fighting troops of all arms must be trained in their use and throughly understand the nature of hand grenade fighting … For success in this, the decisive factors are:- the accuracy, length and quickness of throwing of the individual bombers, and a well arranged supply of grenades. A short but heavy and unexpected volley of grenades is often sufficient to stop the enemy … The cylinder hand grenade with stick has only concussive effect: the egg grenade produces a large number of useful fragments and can be thrown further owing to its more suitable form and smaller weight. Egg grenades, in view of their fragmentation, should be thrown from cover if possible. At the present moment, all the hand grenades used in the German army are time grenades [as distinct from percussion, or explode-on-impact, models].

Distinctly different tactical uses for the grenade were envisaged in attack and defence. For the attack, the key purpose of the grenade was to 'cause the destruction or surrender of the enemy, if he is behind cover where he cannot be reached by rifle fire'. Individual grenadiers were to vary their equipment according to their task, but a standard kit was suggested for most purposes, comprising 'steel helmet; slung rifle or carbine, or pistol; two sandbags containing grenades slung round the neck or both shoulders, or two special hand grenade carriers; entrenching implement; gas helmet; haversack with four iron rations; two water bottles', but 'no valise or pouches' – cartridges being carried more handily in the coat pockets or haversack. All men in an assault group, including the commander, were to carry six to eight stick grenades, or a greater number of the smaller egg bombs; this basic provision to be increased on 'special tasks' or 'where very heavy close fighting is taking place'.

Aggression, with a default of advancing in case of trouble, was key to tactical movement in the attack:

> If it happens that in an attack that the attackers are fired on from a hostile trench beyond hand grenade range, they must all close on the trench at full speed, throwing their grenades, lie down whilst the grenades burst, and then rush into the trench without hesitation. If in the course of this, the men come upon an obstacle which has not been completely destroyed, a continuous stream of hand grenades must be kept up whilst it is being cut. In an attack on special points in the enemy's line, e.g. a flanking emplacement, or in rolling up the enemy working along a trench, only a few men as a rule should throw, the others should supply hand grenades and protect the throwers ... Special enterprises carried out by means of a hand grenade attack e.g. fighting for identifications, occupation of shell craters, capture of a particular piece of trench, seizure of block houses, copses and farms etc. generally require a thorough preparation by the fire of other arms.

Whilst the grenade was arguably the main staple of the attack in trench warfare, it was intended as second fiddle to cartridge weapons in the defence:

To repel an assault, the best weapons are machine guns and rifles. If time [fused] hand grenades are thrown at assaulting infantry, they will not as a rule explode until the enemy has passed beyond them, and so do him no damage. The use of hand grenades becomes valuable only when firearms cannot be employed: or when the enemy has got a lodgment in a dead angle, in shell holes, etc. close to our position, where he cannot be reached by firearms: or when he has broken into our trenches anywhere.

To prepare for such eventualities, skilled bombers were to be placed near likely places, such as the junctions of communication and fire trenches, or alongside trench 'blocks', or near flanking machine guns. A reserve of grenadiers was also to be kept in hand by the company or platoon commander to act as a reserve. To cater for the grenade throwers, watertight boxes of fused bombs were to be laid down in advance, with further supply held in readiness in rear positions.

As far as detailed bombing tactics were concerned, *Nahkampfmittel* suggested that grenades could be used in a wide variety of situations, but that one of the main methods would be for assault groups to work their way along trenches, or through groups of shell holes, throwing as they went. Out of a section of ten or a dozen men, two would be allocated as the main throwers, taking second and third positions behind a lead man armed with rifle or pistol. Those following on behind would include men detailed to watch the flanks, and grenade carriers with fresh supplies of bombs, all ready to take the lead if necessary. The first of the selected bombers would be armed with stick grenades, and would concentrate on throwing one or at most two bays or traverses ahead of the party. The second bomber, using smaller egg bombs, would throw at more distant targets, thus interfering with any enemy attempts to bring up grenades. In attacking a machine gun post or block house, the group would deploy so as to allow one of their own machine guns, or a couple of snipers, 'to keep up an uninterrupted fire on the loopholes of the objective'. Using shell holes or other suitable ground, the remainder now worked 'around the flanks or rear of the enemy, until they get within bombing distance. They then bombard the loopholes and entrances with grenades until the enemy is disabled and the objective can be captured'.

Grenades could also be used in demolition work. Tricks of the trade included wiring the heads of six grenades together on one stick to create a 'concentrated charge' or *geballter Ladung,* which could blow apart large obstacles. In a 'long charge,' grenade heads, with detonators inserted, were attached to a pole or plank about 15cm apart. A couple of men then crawled forward, and either thrust or threw the whole thing into the obstruction, igniting the fuse at an opportune moment. Grenades could similarly be fitted with hooks so that when they were thrown into wire entanglements they caught on, and hung above the ground in the midst of the wire before exploding. As was already common practice, grenade training was to be carried out on a realistic piece of ground, with definite objectives. Amongst the types of throw practised would be lobs over high fences, intended to achieve a good angle of descent; throws from one sap head to another; throws from shell holes; and throws between trees and tree stumps.

The emphasis in *Nahkampfmittel* was definitely on the *Nah,* the near and the personal: the hand-thrown bomb, the dagger, the pistol, the entrenching tool and the bayonet. These were the implements of war that required the attacker to look his adversary in the eye and smite him unhesitatingly at point-blank range. They needed unrelenting determination, and the iron in the soul that Jünger would later eulogise. Faced with such an onslaught, many simply gave up, or ran. Yet the Stormtrooper ethos made demands that some learned they were unhappy to deliver. Sergeant Stefan Westmann made just such a discovery of himself when fighting with 29th Division:

> We got orders to storm the French position. We got in and I saw my comrades start falling to the left and right of me. But then I was confronted by a French Corporal with his bayonet to the ready, just as I had mine. I felt the fear of death in that fraction of a second when I realised that he was after my life, exactly as I was after his. But I was quicker than he was, I pushed his rifle away and ran my bayonet through his chest. He fell, putting his hand on the place where I had hit him, and then I thrust again. Blood came out of his mouth and he died. I nearly vomited. My knees were shaking and they asked me, 'What's the matter with you?' I remembered then that the good

soldier kills without thinking of his adversary as a human being – the very moment he sees him as a fellow man, he's no longer a good soldier. My comrades were absolutely undisturbed by what had happened. One of them boasted that he had killed a *poilu* with the butt of his rifle. Another one had strangled a French captain. A third had hit somebody over the head with his spade. They were ordinary men like me. One was a tram conductor, another a commercial traveller, two were students, the rest farm workers – ordinary people who never would have thought to harm anybody. But I had a dead French soldier in front of me ...

Also described in *Nahkampfmittel* was the use of the *Granatenwerfer*. These *Granatenwerfer*, or bomb throwers, were ideal for use against targets which could not be reached by hand-thrown grenades, having a range of about 300 metres. They were accurate enough to land their projectiles reliably within a rectangle about three to five metres wide and fifty metres long. Given this degree of dispersion, it was recommended that they should be deployed in groups of two to six, ideally dug into positions just behind, or actually in, the front line. Being smaller, the great advantage of the *Granatenwerfer* over the other types of *Minenwerfer*, or mortar, was that it was difficult to detect. The best form of bombardment was achieved when a group of weapons fired off at a rate of about six rounds per minute, thus creating a dense pattern of detonations with the bombs arriving in the target area anything up to 36 times a minute.

In defensive actions, the best use of the *Granatenwerfer* was to fire in order to prevent the enemy from closing on friendly positions, or to harrass the enemy in any trench that he succeeded in taking. In the attack, *Granatenwerfer* barrages were best fired about two or three minutes before the assault went in, particularly where No Man's Land was narrow, making conventional artillery barrages difficult or impossible. Once an attack had been made the weapons were to 'follow up the assaulting columns; they should be dug in, either in the captured line or in adjacent shell holes, to deal with the enemy's rearward lines and to assist in repelling counter-attacks'.

Though pistols were mentioned in *Nahkampfmittel*, the problem of producing a high-powered, close-range weapon for selective clearing of parts of trench systems and bunkers was by no means solved. Grenades were now universal, but obviously they could not be used for really close targets, and the delay of the fuse on most models meant that reaction time could be unacceptably long. There was also a limit to the amount of bombs a man could carry, even if they were of the small 'egg' variety. One answer seemed to be increasing the magazine capacity of existing firearms, thus allowing the soldier to continue shooting whilst advancing through an enemy position without the need to recharge his magazine.

A *Mehrlader*, or high-capacity box, was made for the standard rifle, and does seem to have seen fairly widespread use. However, as a weapon for trench warfare or the assault, its application was limited. The infantryman could indeed continue shooting without having to fill the magazine too frequently, but the device did not materially increase the rate of fire, and the rifle still had the disadvantages of length and difficulty of taking aim in a confined space. Applying the same logic of larger magazines to the P08 'Luger' semi-automatic pistol appeared to offer better dividends. Indeed, being semi-automatic, it was already a much quicker arm to shoot than the bolt-action rifle. Tests showed that a trained man could easily discharge the eight rounds it held within five seconds, replacing the magazine in another five. Eight rounds could thus be delivered, and the pistol reloaded, in a time that a rifleman would be hard pressed to shoot half that number. The fact that the pistol shot a relatively short-range 9mm round was of no account when the target was close.

So it was that a 32-round *Trommel*, or drum magazine, was introduced. The general idea for such a magazine had first been floated as early as 1911 by Austro-Hungarian inventors Tatarek and von Benko, and an improved version for the 9mm parabellum cartridge was patented by Friedrich Blum two years later. Now its time appeared to have come. At least limited issue was made of a complete kit consisting of a long-barrelled *Lange* Luger pistol, two 32-round magazines and a simple wooden shoulder stock. According to its manual, the pistol was normally worn in its holster with a strap over the shoulder, whilst the large magazines were carried in bags on the waist belt. In this configuration, the pistol effectively became a small, rapid-firing, high-capacity carbine. There were also experimental attempts to make the pistol into a 'machine pistol', that is one, capable of full automatic fire. Whilst an ingenious concept, various practical difficulties interposed. Tests of 1914, carried out by two Mexican brothers, had shown that the gun could be made automatic, but it emptied so quickly as to be uncontrollable, and defeated the whole object of the enterprise. Heinrich Senn of Switzerland achieved much the same result in 1916, and only cured the fault by the rather ludicrous provision of a bipod. Futher experiment came up with a rifle-type stock for a fully automatic pistol which was demonstrated to a ministry commission in December 1917.

This was not adopted, but the concept of a short-barrelled gun with a large-capacity magazine filled with pistol-sized cartridges and capable of full automatic fire was a good one. Hugo Schmeisser's 'machine pistol' MP 18 had just these characteristics, combining an action firing at a manageable 400 rounds per minute cyclic rate with a shoulder stock and the familiar drum magazine. Surviving instructions suggest that it was intended to issue this *Kugelspritz*, or 'bullet squirter', to officers, NCOs, one man in ten in assault companies, and to small squads within other units. Surviving photographs from training sessions show the MP18 being used to lead squads along trenches during clearing. It proved accurate and useful to a range of about 50 metres in moving battle. The weapon undoubtably had some impact, but only about 30,000 were manufactured before the end of hostilities. The Allies clearly thought that they were significant, or at least had significant potential, because they were not allowed to be retained by the German army following defeat.

Countering Tanks

It was arguably only in 1917 that it was actually realised what a serious problem tanks might be – particularly as, at this time, the German army was not blessed with any except for those that they could capture from the British or French. Never would Germany succeed in producing tanks in any numbers during the course of the First World War, and the only recourse was to seek methods of nullifying what to many infantrymen was a terrifying threat.

Following the first use of the tank on the Somme on 15 September 1916, German reactions appear to have been divided into two distinct camps: those who had been on the receiving end and were concerned, if not terrified; and those who had not seen a tank, nor any significant breakthrough resulting from their use, and were therefore inclined to warn against overreaction.

There was no doubt which group Private Gustav Ebelshauser of 17th Bavarian regiment fell into. He recorded in his memoirs that as soon as the first tanks hove into view, there was consternation and cries of warning:

> It was a useless shriek of alarm. The whole front was aware of the oncoming steel monsters. 'Steel monsters' – the words came out of their mouths in spite of themselves. What were these things? Facing them they did not know what to do. Could they really offer any opposition? Was it not better to flee? Was it not folly to sacrifice so many lives by trying to hold the position? The monsters' motors hummed and droned louder as they crawled increasingly nearer. They advanced relentlessly, up, down, closer and closer. Holes, hills, rocks, even barbed wire meant nothing. They pursued their goal in a straight line, levelling everything in their passage. The men began to shoot, but rifle and machine gun bullets could do no damage. The iron beasts were still approaching. There seemed to be no possible escape except for a wild retreat ... The men were ready, waiting. This time their grenades hit the sides and roof of the steel carcass, but it kept on moving. Then came great confusion and chaos. The defending line broke. Some remained, others rushed forward toward the beast, still others ran in the opposite direction. Machine guns rattled and screams filled the air. Terror stricken, Ebelshauser and his comrades seemed nailed to their places. They had wanted to flee, now their legs trembled, refusing support. They watched the advancing group. Bending forward, one following the other, they reached the monster. They immediately divided, two for each caterpillar. Grenades were thrown through small apertures. They then took cover running back as fast as they could. Five or six were shot and fell to the ground. But the machine had been brought to a stop. If nothing else this caused one or two in the vicinity to turn back.

The 77th Infantry Regiment had, if anything, a worse experience. At Thiepval a few days later, some of its men managed to clamber on top of a tank seeking out chinks in the enemy armour, but on this occasion there were none to be found. As their regimental historian, quoted in Duffy's *Through German Eyes*, observed, they might as well have been 'attacking a battleship with spades'. German intelligence took a contrary view, a paper of 5 October 1916 attributing the successes of the tank essentially to its novelty. Part of the trouble was that it took a surprisingly long time to get firm information on the specification and precise appearance of the beasts which assailed them. Some troops who got fleeting glances and fled gave wildly inaccurate accounts; the difference between 'male' and 'female' tanks with their various armaments was at first thought to be far greater than it was, and some misinterpreted the pieces of wreckage scattered by heavy shell fire in No Man's Land.

What became clear fairly rapidly was that the best antidote to armour was artillery and plenty of it. This could take the form of a barrage fired on the general area: shells and mortar bombs causing damage either by catastrophic direct hits on upper decking; or by near misses, which blew off tracks and steering gear, concussed the crew, and formed craters which were difficult to negotiate. Fire 'over open sights' could be even more devastating, a single well-placed round blowing a tank to pieces, but artillery crews indulging in such heroics exposed themselves to all manner of return fire if not well concealed. In the light of experience gained, a *Merkblatt*, or 'explanatory leaflet', prepared by 2nd Army in January 1917 gave much more accurate details of the British tank and its vulnerabilities. Red areas on diagrams marked out the viable *Angriffspunkte*, or suitable 'attack points' for the infantry, which included vision ports, hatches and certain areas around the sponsons. 'SmK', or steel-cored bullets from rifles and machine guns could be used profitably, as could multiple grenade charges. Perhaps best of all was the light *Minenwerfer*, now attached to infantry units, as it was capable both of armour penetration and damaging tracks.

A detailed report and instruction prepared by 27th Division that April gave a considered view of the capabilities of enemy tanks and the methods that could be used to stop them:

Ordinary wire entanglements are easily overcome by the tanks. Where there are high, dense and broad entanglements such as those in front of the Siegfried [Hindenburg] line, the wire is apt to get entangled in the tracks of the tanks. On April 11th one tank was hopelessly stuck in our wire entanglement. Deep trenches, even eight feet wide, seem to be a serious obstacle to tanks. At long ranges by day, tanks will be engaged by all batteries that can deliver fire with observation that are not occupied with other more important tasks. All kinds of batteries put tanks out of action on April 11th. Battery commanders must be permitted to act upon their own initiative to the fullest possible extent ... April 11th proved that rifle and machine gun fire with armour-piercing ammunition can put tanks out of action. Fire directed at the sides of the tanks is more effective than fire at the fore end. The greatest danger for the tanks is the ready inflammability of the fuel and oil tanks. Machine gun fire is capable of igniting them. The garrison of the trench will take cover behind the traverses and will direct their fire at the hostile infantry following the tanks; firing on tanks with ordinary small arms ammunition is useless. Anti-tank guns are indispensable; they are particularly useful for combating tanks which have penetrated our lines and are within our front lines; however anti-tank guns are a source of danger to our own infantry.

At the same time that tactics were assessed to see what might and might not work, artillery was reorganised in such a way as to have maximum chance of stopping the tank incursions. 'Infantry guns', which had already been the subject of assault-troop experiment, were seized upon as offering distinct advantages. First of all, they were generally small and thus relatively easy to handle, and not easy for the enemy to detect. Second, being allotted to the infantry, they were dispersed at, or near to, the front line, and could be positioned so as to screen areas against breakthrough. Where ordinary batteries of field guns were concerned, a useful measure was to allot one as a 'close defence' piece, perhaps positioning it so as to cover the most likely avenues of advance upon the battery.

Whilst infantry attacks on tanks using grenades were sometimes successful, to do this required extreme bravery on the part of the soldier. In getting to within a few yards of armoured vehicles many were killed, and there was still no guarantee of inflicting damage serious enough to stop the tank. The defensive armour of tanks was being improved all the time, so there was also a limit to what steel-cored bullets could be expected to achieve. Putting a weapon in the hands of the infantry that would balance this unequal combat was therefore a high priority. Obviously, the tank was a big, heavy target, so a big, heavy rifle might provide the answer. Thus began a whole new type of weapon: the 'anti-tank rifle', or to the Germans, the *Tank-Gewehr* or *T-Gewehr*. The Mauser anti-tank rifle was perfected and deployed by 1918, and was indeed a hugely scaled-up, single-shot, bolt-action rifle. It weighed 17kg, fired a 13mm round, and had massive recoil; it was thus required to be fired from its bipod, or at least firmly rested on a solid surface. Cumbersome as it was, the *T-Gewehr* had sufficient performance for the intended target; being capable of penetrating 25mm of armour at 100 metres, or about 15mm at twice this range. Given its weight, it was best used defensively, with the gunner tracking the target, or waiting for a tank to cross a predetermined field of fire.

The *T-Gewehr* appears to have reached the front-line troops in at least small numbers in the early summer, and was certainly encountered by the Australian Corps and accompanying tanks at the battle of Hamel on 4 July. The new Mark V tanks performed well, being observed to run over and crush several German machine guns and their detachments. Two anti-tank rifles were captured, but at this stage British intelligence professed to be unimpressed by the gun, pronouncing it 'a very clumsy weapon', which might, however, 'be developed'. Five tanks were disabled out of the sixty-four used in the battle – a fairly low total – but whether any of these were victims of the *T-Gewehr* does not appear to have been recorded. The best antidote to the antidote, predictably enough, was thought to be artillery in the shape of a creeping barrage which could deal with anti-tank rifle teams just before the arrival of tanks.

1. The propaganda image of the heroic and resilient Stormtrooper from Professor Fritz Erler's famous poster issued in March 1917. The text reads, 'Help us Conquer! Subscribe to the War Loan'.

Above: **2.** Pre-war infantry manoeuvres. The basic formation is a thick line with the officers to the fore.

Left: **3.** Soldier of *Landwehr* Infantry Regiment Nr 29, in full marching order, *c.*1914. The Mauser rifle has a five-round magazine, and the 1909 ammunition pouches worn on the belt have a capacity of 120 rounds. The *Landwehr* was a second line of trained reserves composed mainly of men over the age of twenty-seven, called out to support the active army and reserve formations in time of need.

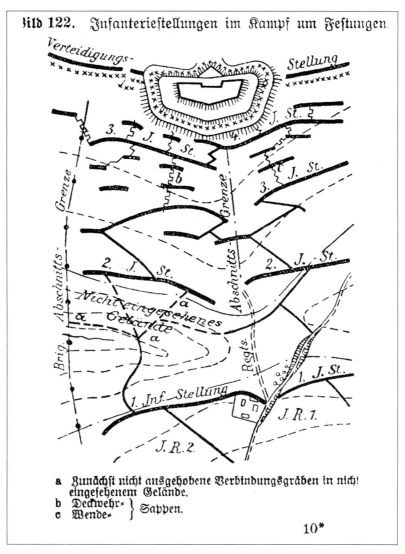

Bild 122. Infanteriestellungen im Kampf um Festungen.

a Zunächst nicht ausgehobene Verbindungsgräben in nicht eingesehenem Gelände.
b Deckwehr- } Sappen.
c Wende- }

10*

4. The use of trenches in the fight against fortifications, as depicted in the official manual *Feld-Pionierdienst aller Waffen* of December 1911. It was expected that trenches would have at least a limited role in future war, but attack rather than defence would be the requirement for swift victory.

dabei den Schützengraben nach Möglichkeit der Sicht zu entziehen, wird die Brustwehr so niedrig gehalten, wie es Geländeform, Bewachsung und Bodenverhältnisse

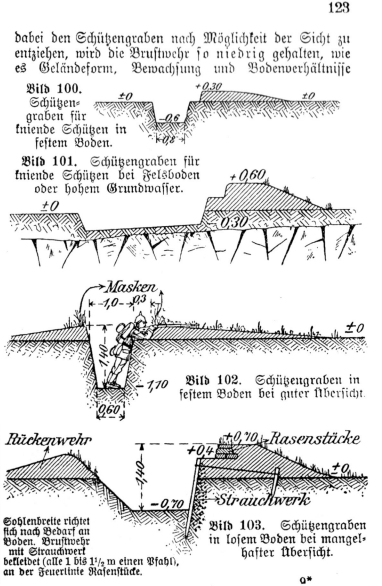

Bild 100. Schützengraben für kniende Schützen in festem Boden.

Bild 101. Schützengraben für kniende Schützen bei Felsboden oder hohem Grundwasser.

Bild 102. Schützengraben in festem Boden bei guter Übersicht.

Bild 103. Schützengraben in losem Boden bei mangelhafter Übersicht.

Sohlenbreite richtet sich nach Bedarf an Boden. Brustwehr mit Strauchwerk bekleidet (alle 1 bis 1½ m einen Pfahl), an der Feuerlinie Rasenstücke.

5. Standard German trench profiles for different ground conditions, from *Feld-Pionierdienst aller Waffen.* Trench digging was affected by topography, but most trenches adhered to preordained patterns in their essentials.

Ich hatt' einen Kameraden.
Will mir die Hand noch reichen,
Dieweil ich eben lad.

6. The 'brisk merry war' of popular imagination with flags and drums, as depicted on a sentimental postcard. The words *Ich hatt' einen Kameraden* (I had a comrade), are from a song commonly played at military funerals.

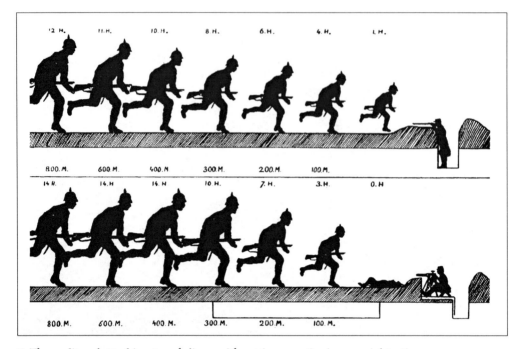

7. The reality of attacking trench lines without 'preparation' or special tactics as explained in the French publication *Sur le Vif* of January, 1915. Riflemen whittle away most of the superior numbers of attackers before they can reach the trench. With machine guns added to their torment the attacking infantry are unlikely to reach the enemy at all.

Herr
gib
ihm
die
ewige
Ruhe

Und
das
ewige
Licht
leuchte
ihm.

Zum frommen Andenken im Gebete an
unsern lieben unverg. Sohn, Bruder und
Paten

Heinrich Feulner

Inf. b. 20. Res. Inf. Rgt.. 12. Komp. Geb.
am 14. Dez. 1894 zu Schlegelhard.
Gest. den Heldentod fürs Vaterland am
25. Sept. 1915 in Beaucamps bei Arras
(Amentieres).

Beim heißen Kampf im Feindesland
Traf dich die Todesstunde;
Die Lieben dein im Heimatland
Traf schwer die bitt're Kunde,
Den Heldentod für's Vaterland,
Bist Liebster du gestorben,
Hast mutig dir mit tap'frer Hand
Den Himmelslohn erworben.

O liebster Jesus! Um Deines bitteren
Leidens willen erbarme dich seiner
und aller armen Seelen.

8. Infantryman Heinrich Feulner, 'died a hero's death for the fatherland' at Beauchamps near Arras in September 1915, aged 20. About two million Germans would be killed in World War I; the vast majority of them in the army, and the vast majority of those in the infantry.

9. Some of the types of German grenade in use in 1915. The stick, or *Stiel*, hand grenades either side are of the first model without caps at the ends of the wooden handles. The segmented ball is the *Kugel* grenade of 1913, and in the centre is a 1913 *Discus*, explode-on-impact type. The tins are simple 'emergency' patterns, similar models of which were produced by a number of nations.

10. Pioneer stores behind the line at Neuville, March 1916. The equipment held here includes grenades, explosives, and on the bench to the left a 1915 model *Granatenwerfer*, or bomb thrower.

11. Throwing grenades from a trench, 1915. This bomber wears the soft *Feldmutze* or field cap, and has removed one of his ammunition pouches, allowing two additional stick grenades to be suspended by their hooks from his belt.

12. The penalties of a strong enemy and poor tactics: German dead litter the battlefield in a photograph reproduced at Weimar in June 1915. The boots of the dead were commonly removed as reusable salvage.

13. *Handgranten* or *Stosstrupp*,
probably early 1916. The men are festooned with grenades, and carry equipment
to allow the rapid creation of a 'trench block' to help hold the ground captured by
bombing along trenches. Light 'assault packs' and early type soft gas mask cases are
also worn. The spikes have been removed from the *Pickelhauben* in accordance with
orders of late 1915.

Pionier in voller Ausrüstung.

14. The 'pioneer in full equipment' from
a cartoon reproduced in Cologne, 1916.
Whilst attacking was best done lightly
equipped the volume of new stores
threatened to engulf the fighting man.

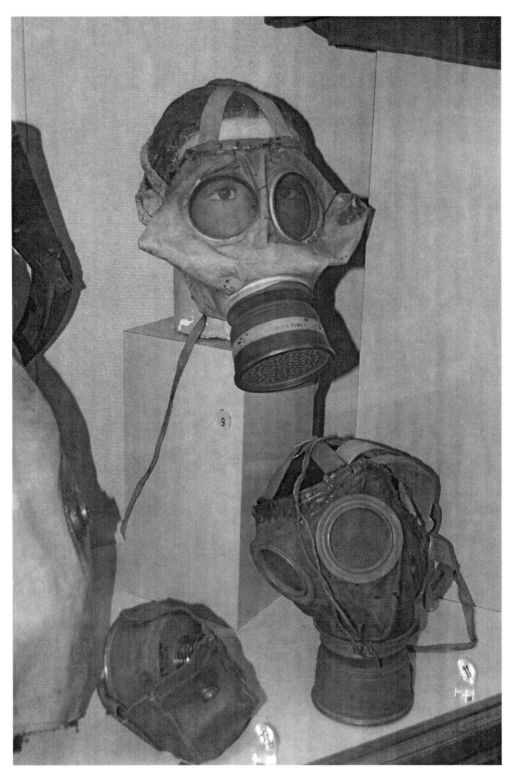

15. The two major models of German gas mask: top, the rubberised fabric type introduced in 1915, and bottom, the 1917 mask of sheep leather.

16. A large-model flame-thrower in the act of discharge, *c.*1917. The large flame-thrower used 100-litre tanks of fuel and commonly required a crew of three. Though they were spectacular in effect they had less tactical mobility than the small, backpack models which were capable of leading infantry attacks.

Opposite below: **18.** Trench system in a wooded area showing walkways, fire steps, and bays with supplies of grenades ready to repel attack. Rifles and machine guns were the weapon of preference where there was adequate field of fire; grenades could be used for close range groups, or lobbed into places that were otherwise 'dead zones'.

17. The application of ever greater destructive power: a 21cm *Morser* and its wicker-covered shells on the Eastern Front. Though *Morser* may be translated as 'mortar', the 21cm was effectively a huge, short-barrelled howitzer with a maximum range of about 10,000 metres. A single shell weighed about 120kg.

Dornstellung

19. Troops in a deep bunker from Elk Eber's painting *Sie Trommeln*, which translates as 'they drum' – a reference to 'drum' or heavy barrage fire by the enemy. Bunkers saved lives but the occupants, if lucky enough to emerge, could be hungry, thirsty, disorientated or even shellshocked by the time they appeared. Bold attackers might succeed in sealing the exits or throwing in grenades.

DUGOUT WITH OBSERVATION POST

REINFORCED CONCRETE - EARLY TYPE .WITH UNIFORM ROD REINFORCEMENT

From the Official Manual STELLUNGSBAU, 2ⁿᵈ Edition, 15 Dec.1916

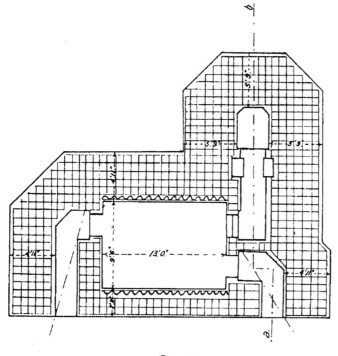

— PLAN —

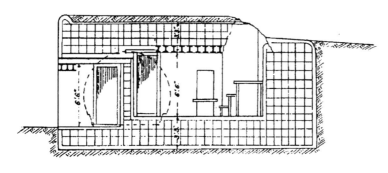

SECTION A.B.

Drawn by F.G.Newcomb. 2ⁿᵈ Cpl. R.E.

20. Reinforced concrete dugout copied from a type shown in the official German manual *Stellungsbau*. Such works were not only strong enough to withstand direct hits from smaller shells, but could be made sufficiently shallow to allow the defenders to make an easy exit when needed.

German Mashien Gun

21. Breech and belt-feed detail of the MG 08 machine gun; scourge of the Allied infantry. Imaginative machine gun deployment allowed increasingly economic use of troops in the trenches and inflicted punishing losses on any attack. Nevertheless the MG 08 and its mount were extremely heavy.

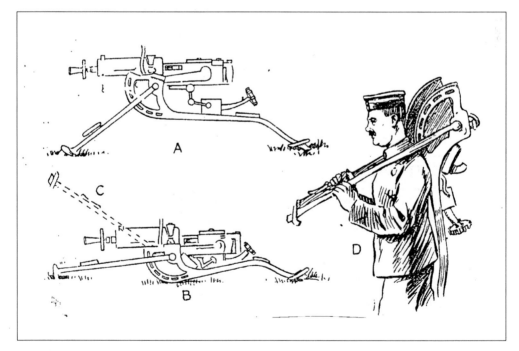

22. Contemporary sketches showing: (A) the set up position of the MG 08 and sledge mount (B) mount adjusted to carry like a stretcher (C) front legs adjusted for dragging, and (D) the mount carried on the shoulders. It took a strong man and good ground conditions to move the gun at all by himself, so usually the weapon was 'stretchered' between two, three or four men.

23. The MG 08 used with an extemporised light 'trench mount'. The team is led by an NCO with binoculars. Two men fire and feed the gun, the remainder are spare men and ammunition carriers.

24. A four-man MG 08/15 light machine gun *Trupp*. Though heavier than the enemy equivalents the MG 08/15 finally gave the infantry its own mobile fire support, allowing genuine independent tactical use of platoons and squads in the attack.

25. Drawing from an inter-war publication showing MG 08/15 light machine guns being rapidly moved into position to counter enemy infantry. Surprise fire from a flank was often even more effective than emplaced machine guns because it enfiladed enemy formations and was extremely difficult to combat.

GUT STURM!

26. 'Attack hard!' A poster designed by Andreas Paul Weber, an illustrator who also produced work for the Leipzig *Illustrated Times*. The Stormtrooper, complete with grenade bag, rushes on as though on the wing of an eagle.

27. *From left to right:* Hindenburg, Chief of the General Staff, the Kaiser, and Ludendorff, the First Quartermaster General at General Headquarters, January 1917. Following the debacle of Verdun and the accession of Hindenburg, German industry and population were focused ever more single-mindedly on victory.

28. *Nahkampfmittel*: Some close-range weaponry with a steel helmet. The distinctive *Stahlhelm* was first developed experimentally in late 1915 and introduced in 1916 as a reaction to the large number of head wounds, some of which were caused by surprisingly small or slow-moving fragments. Its distinctive side lugs allowed the fitting of a brow plate. Two versions of the 9mm 'Luger' pistol are shown: foreground, the standard model 1908 with its short barrel and eight round magazine, and the *Lange* type with its long barrel. This latter is fitted with a high-capacity 'snail' magazine. The 1915 model stick grenade has a 5.5-second time delay.

Above: **29.** Defenders of the *Wotan Stellung,* a third-line position near Arras, in a not terribly convincing pose. Two of the troops are ready to toss grenades out over the top, another man emerging from the dugout entrance carries a *Leuchtpistole,* or 'light pistol', by means of which coloured flare signals could be given.

31. An assault troop officer armed not only with stick grenades and carbine, but a 'concentrated charge' with seven grenade heads wired together for the destruction of obstacles, bunkers and even tanks. The model-1916 metal shield with rotating shutter was particularly useful when camouflaged as part of a fixed position.

Opposite below: **30.** A light *Minenwerfer* section, pictured in mid 1917. Light trench mortars or *Minenwerfer* gave attacking troops the ability to carry forward with them genuine trench-busting weapons. This model, capable of firing gas as well as conventional high-explosive bombs, had a range of about 1200 metres, and was discharged by a pull on a lanyard. It could also be towed along by the team on a wheeled carriage.

32. Infantryman, 1918. This veteran wears the *Bluse,* or concealed-button simplified jacket, introduced in 1915. His decorations include the ribbon of the Iron Cross, second class, and the wound badge award. This badge, or *Abzeichen Fur Verwundete,* showing a steel helmet and crossed swords, was introduced by the Kaiser on 3 March 1918, and authorised by the King of Bavaria just over a week later. For one or two wounds the badge was black; for three or four, silver; and for five or more, gold.

33. A 21cm *Morser* seen at Licourt on the Western Front. Deeply emplaced and cunningly camouflaged the weapon is loaded by means of four men offering up the shell on a litter.

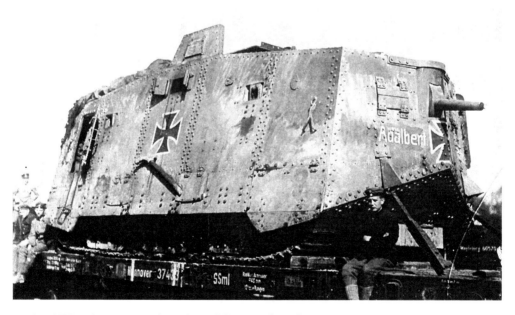

34. An A7V tank in transit aboard a rail flat car. Though some Allied tanks were captured, no German tanks would be made until 1918 – and even then there were pitifully few, hugely outnumbered by superior British and French types. Lack of tanks created a significant void in German tactical development.

Left: **35.** German soldiers operate an MG 08 against aircraft in the Vosges area. By the latter part of the war ground attack aircraft, as well as reconnaissance craft, were fully integrated into the attack plan. Anti-aircraft weaponry was a concern of both the artillery and infantry.

Below: **36.** Stormtroop attack over shell holes. The troops carry grenade bags, and have slung carbines – more handy weapons than the full-length rifle. This is a loose knot of men, moving as fast as possible and taking cover where they find it, not a pedestrian line.

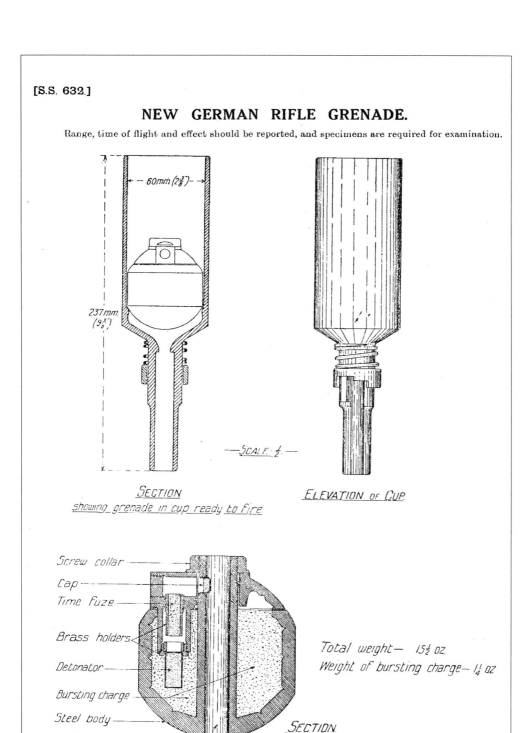

[S.S. 632.]

NEW GERMAN RIFLE GRENADE.

Range, time of flight and effect should be reported, and specimens are required for examination.

— 60mm (2⅜″) —

237mm (9⅜″)

— SCALE ¼ —

SECTION
showing grenade in cup ready to fire

ELEVATION OF CUP.

Screw collar
Cap
Time fuze

Brass holders
Detonator
Bursting charge
Steel body
Cylindrical passage for bullet

Total weight — 15½ oz.
Weight of bursting charge — 1¼ oz

SECTION
— FULL SIZE —

37. A British diagram of the final model of German rifle grenade produced during the war. The small 'jam pot' type bomb is slid into a cup discharger on the end of the rifle. A bullet from the gun passes through a channel in the bomb, both launching it and igniting its time fuse.

38. The complete family of German trench mortars in use in the latter part of the war: light, medium, and heavy, all on their wheeled carriages. Four shells are shown, including short and long rounds for the heavy weapon.

Opposite: **39.** Cover illustration from Johannes Theuerkrauff's *Aufposten vor der Siegfriedstellung,* or 'outposts beyond the Hindenburg line', an official publication of the Nazi *Kulturgemeinde* extolling the virtues of those who shielded the retreat to the Hindenburg line in 1917.

Johannes Theuerkauff

Auf Posten vor der Siegfriedstellung

Hermann Hillger Verlag, Berlin W9 und Leipzig
Nr. 615

Und setzet ihr nicht das Leben ein/nie
wird euch das Leben gewonnen sein

FR·V·SCHILLER·

Linolschnitt von Georg Sluyterman v. Langeweyde

40. Illustration from one of a set of patriotic field postcards produced
by artists Sluyterman and Langwede, and published by Kuster of Essen
in 1940. The quotation from Schiller encourages the new generation of
troops to hazard their lives as bravely as the *Frontsoldaten* of World War I.

8

1918: Birth of a Legend

What is commonly regarded as the ultimate Stormtrooper bible finally appeared on 1 January 1918 as *Der Angriff im Stellungskrieg*, or 'The Attack in Position Warfare', being 'Part 14 (Provisional)' of the 'Manual of Position Warfare for All Arms'. Amendments would be added on 26 January and 27 July. Undoubtedly, this was the highest expression of the doctrine of *Stoss*, or shock, tactics, and that which ultimately affected the course of the 1918 offensives most directly; but as we have seen, it was just the last in a line of similar papers. Many of its parts had already been published in other forms, and many of its ideas had already been employed, and not only by German forces. Its signal significance was, however, that like the British *Training and Employment of Divisions*, issued within days of the German document, it brought together the best of what had been developed over the past three years into a single, universal instruction. Arguably, it put together many things that had been widely used for limited objectives, and produced a rounded formula for use, writ large, in the *Angriffschlacht*, or 'attack offensive'. In many ways, this would prove seminal, and very successful – a model to be emulated. But as part of the wider strategy of 1918, given Germany's very limited window of opportunity and weakening position, the final result would be disaster.

The man mainly credited with *Der Angriff im Stellungskrieg* was a relatively junior officer of the Operations Section of the General Staff, *Hauptmann* Hermann Geyer: an officer whom Ludendorff would describe in his memoirs as possessing 'a well-developed sense of tactics and a clear mode of expression'. He did not, however, start from anything like a blank canvas, and the evidence points both to input from many others, and to study of previous literature. Moreover, Colonel Max Bauer, Geyer's superior officer in the Operations Section, appears to have shown both fairness and generosity in giving Geyer suitable credit. Bauer and Geyer had previously worked together on other tactical documents, notably *The Principles of Command in Defensive Battle* of December 1916. As so often, Bauer's influence was pervasive, and may be traced back as far as his pre-war association with Ludendorff. Still, Geyer's penmanship was better and he had the opportunity to concentrate on one thing at a time, whilst Bauer's higher office and febrile mind drew him away in many other directions.

Ludendorff himself had already canvassed commanding generals for submissions to inform the 1918 manual of attack, but there was plenty of other material about to inspire the new work. These included the various attack instructions, and the examinations of French and British methods all the way back to March 1915; specialised manuals on the use of, amongst other things, artillery, gas, flame-throwers and *Nahkampfmittel*; and a wide range of 'Lessons Drawn' papers, some of which were taken from the example of the Battle of the Somme in 1916. Doubtless, Geyer also used the 1917 *Lessons from Offensive Enterprises*, which drew particular attention to Riga, but this is not at all the same as saying that the methods outlined in *Der Angriff im Stellungskrieg* were developed at Riga, or indeed on the Eastern Front in general. Indeed, if we are to take Ludendorff's own remarks at face value, the drive for innovation was made mainly in the West: 'On the Eastern Front we had for the most part adhered to the old tactical methods and old training which we had learned in the days of peace. Here [in the West] we met with new conditions and it was my duty to adapt myself to them'.

Nor can we even reasonably suggest that Georg Bruchmüller's artillery methods used in 1918 were developed mainly at, or for, the Riga battle. He had a track record of success back to 1915, had already been outstanding at the Battle of Lake Naroch in early 1916, and had certainly been recognised for his groundbreaking work by early 1917. This was so much so that he received the prestigious *Pour le Mérite*, or 'Blue Max', on 1 May 1917 – a full four months before von Hutier's Eighth Army crossed the Dvina to crush Russian resistance in the celebrated two-day battle at Riga. This engagement was certainly an impressive success, but one that needs certain qualification. As has been pointed out, by September 1917 the Russians were not far from their final collapse. Perhaps more importantly, they had realised a German attack in this area was brewing, and had withdrawn some of their forces accordingly. It was also the case that the most innovative feature of the Riga attack was actually the river assault crossing and the rapid erection of pontoon bridges by the engineers. Neither of these aspects would have particular relevance to what happened on the Western Front a few months later.

What can be conclusively proved is that in writing the new attack document, Geyer referred to other sections of the *Manual of Position Warfare*, published before January 1918, notably those on artillery; more general artillery and infantry manuals; and to a document entitled 'The Mounting of Minor Offensive Operations in the Vailly Group in May and June 1917'. All these are mentioned in the text of *Der Angriff im Stellungskrieg*. Riga is mentioned just once, in a section on changes in weather, along with Verdun, Romania and Italy. Moreover, explicit reference to Riga was not part of the original edition, but forms part of an amendment. A good number of the ideas finally set down in the new instruction had indeed already been tried out in the west, for those who cared to notice them. As the British *Official History* description of the German counter-attack at Cambrai in late 1917 makes clear:

> Preceded by patrols the Germans had advanced at 7 a.m. in small columns bearing many light machine guns, and, in some cases flame-throwers. From overhead low flying airplanes, in greater numbers than had hitherto been seen, bombed and machine-gunned the British defenders, causing further casualties and, especially, distraction at the critical moment. Nevertheless few posts appear to have been attacked from the front, the assault sweeping in between to envelop them from flanks and rear.

Ernst Jünger speaks explicitly of training his assault company in early 1918 with live bombs and bullets, in order to 'turn to account the lessons', not of Riga, but 'of the Cambrai battle'.

The message is clear: Geyer did not work alone, and the influence of Eastern Front operations was just one strand of many brought together in *Der Angriff im Stellungskrieg*, which was a wide-ranging synthesis that became more than the sum of its parts. It may be argued that the new manual was the best, boldest and most far-reaching of its type, but it showed considerable elements of similarity with a number of Allied publications of the same period. Key concepts included the thorough 'education' of the assaulting troops, the role of command, the quality of inter-arm liaison and a 'centre of gravity' to the attack. Naturally, troops were to be thoroughly trained and practised in attacking 'trenches specially constructed for the purpose', but they were also to be educated 'in that spirit of bold attack and will to conquer, with which we entered the present war' and which was 'the first guarantee of success'. Command during the attack in position warfare was not simply a matter of giving clear orders and ensuring co-operation between all arms and neighbouring sectors, but recognising and taking advantage of the fact that 'every attack offers an opportunity for independent decision and action even down to the private soldier'. Close liaison between all arms was not seen as just tactically important, but as vital for informing the decisions of higher command, and preventing surprises from the flanks. The idea of a 'centre of gravity', or *Schwerpunkt*, was not new but ancient, and helped to ensure a superiority of force at a vital point where a modest success might produce results disproportionate to its effort.

Unlike some more limited efforts, the new manual purported to outline both local thrusts and full-scale offensive battle, 'leading from position warfare to the breakthrough' – the holy grail of 'open warfare'. Indeed, it suggested that tactical penetration could be developed into a 'strategical breakthrough'. In so doing, the attacker would have to take account of the likelihood that the defender would pour fresh troops into counter-attacks. The 'breakthrough battle' was therefore characterised by 'penetration to the furthest possible objective', including capture of the enemy artillery on the first day, consolidation of gains, the bringing up of both fresh infantry and 'the mass of artillery … devouring the series of hostile positions … rapidly and in depth'. In this limited respect, the new German doctrine was reminiscent of Captain Andre Laffargue's admonition, made in 1915, that enemy positions should be 'swallowed in a single gulp'. Nevertheless, Laffargue had far more in common with what failed in 1916 than with what succeeded in 1918.

Der Angriff im Stellungskrieg further postulated that though attack in depth suggested that each assaulting division would be best deployed on a fairly narrow front, this would not be less than 2000 metres for each three regiment division, and as much as 3000 metres might be allotted for more limited attacks. Amendments to the first edition added the advice that putting in powerful and adequate artillery was more likely to stimulate further advance after the initial assault than fresh infantry. Reserves were to be pushed in explicitly 'where the attack is proceeding well'. New divisions were not usually to relieve the old, but 'interpolated between other divisions', so generating a fan-shaped extension of the attack, spreading into the rear of the enemy position.

Preparation for the attack was to be thorough but subtle so as to keep the enemy in ignorance of its place and strength. Having learned their trade against dummy positions, divisions would be insinuated forward by stages to the vital sector. Staffs and command posts would be established first, and supply lines worked out. Then a 'skeleton establishment' could be formed, which would be 'clothed' as subsequent groups came up from their training. Supplies were to be dumped with as little evidence to the opposition as possible, 'in numerous depots well forward'.

The role of the artillery was seen as crucial, and was necessarily to be co-ordinated at divisional, corps and army level. Preparatory fire was not to be protracted or indiscriminate, but aimed at producing specific objectives in a short time span: 'concentrated in time and space'. For minor and medium-sized enterprises the opening bombardment might be as short as a few minutes, with some hours being required for major operations. The battle tasks of the artillery were sevenfold. Three of these tasks were essentially preparatory, being: the neutralisation of enemy artillery and mortars; the neutralisation of trench garrisons and destruction of positions; and the bombardment of reserves and communications. Four further objectives were foreseen in the support of the attack: producing 'creeping' barrages; pushing forward 'infantry guns' and field artillery with the advancing troops; shooting protective barrages to defend infantry on captured positions; and repelling counter-attacks. Trench mortars were an integral part of the plan, being exceptionally well suited to preparatory bombardment of enemy trenches and engaging enemy mortars. In deep break-throughs, each infantry battalion would have two light *Minenwerfer* teams attached, and a horsed medium *Minenwerfer* company, with two or three ammunition carts accompanying each mortar, would be used as a divisional unit.

The type of ammunition used by guns and mortars would be varied as to its task, gas shelling being seen as particularly use-ful for the neutralisation of enemy batteries. In this instance, the primary effect would not be high levels of fatality, or the destruc-tion of the enemy guns, but temporary suppression whilst enemy gunners struggled to don their masks and cleared the injured from their positions. Thus it was that gas suppression was seen as essen-tially temporary and something which might well need repeating during operations on longer time frames. In bombarding trenches, the common method was to allot target sectors to each battery, with a howitzer battery on every hundred metres of trench line. Where possible, trench bombardments were fired from a flank, thereby increasing the possibility of shells pitching directly into the trench. Heavy and super-heavy guns would be directed wherever possible onto the deep dugouts, machine gun positions and the like. Trench mortars would be concentrated on the nearest enemy positions.

It would seldom be practicable to 'annihilate all living resistance' in a given area, but it would be possible to cause loss, which would make the enemy 'keep his head down' and shake morale. Moreover, communications could be disrupted and observation impaired 'so that he may finally be surprised by the movement of the infantry attack' and thrown into confusion. Success would depend on the attacking infantry not allowing the effect of the bombardment to wear off, but taking immediate advantage. Though it would rarely happen that the attacking infantry were entirely spared from 'hand-to-hand fighting' it would, however, be light 'if the infantry makes a really determined attack and presses forward so rapidly that the leading men reach the defenders simultaneously with the last rounds from their own guns'. Artillery fire was never to be allowed to become 'rigidly regular', thus allowing the enemy to take advantage of predictable lulls. Various tricks to be employed included crescendos of *Trommel*, or 'drum', fire in the bombardment, for lowering of morale, and sudden bursts of fire to catch the unwary. Lengthening range and pauses were calculated to make the enemy think attack was imminent.

Perhaps the most problematic element in the breakthrough battle was to bring forward the artillery with enough ammunition over the ground seized by the infantry. For this purpose, some of the batteries at least would remain unused in the first action, or rested for a period. They would then move over the battlefield as swiftly as possible, helped along by the provision of bridging materials and parties of engineers to smooth their path. A proportion of the artillery, as for example the light *Minenwerfer* and one field battery per infantry regiment, was to be used as 'accompanying artillery'. This would move up abreast with the advancing infantry, opening fire 'at close range over open sights'.

The infantry battle was not seen as a calculation of attributing simple numerical strengths to either side, and assuming the stronger would prevail. Rather it was a matter of comparative 'fighting power (which depends on rest, training and equipment), the care taken in preparation and the skill of officers and men, combined with rapid and determined action'. Wherever possible, the attacking infantry were to be given short distances to traverse in reaching the enemy lines; to do this they could gather in trenches, craters and dugouts, but 'jumping off' positions were not to be made obvious to the enemy for fear of attracting shelling. Short distances would both reduce casualties and reduce the numbers required to achieve an objective. In all events, the numbers of infantry gathered in any one spot was to be kept to the number needed for the task, overcrowding simply leading to additional losses.

Naturally, large attacks would mean having to cross the enemy's barrage zone, but the destructive effects of this could be mitigated by suitable tactics. Surprise would mean that at least part of the first wave could 'escape part of the hostile barrage', therefore the first wave would be relatively thick, but would advance distributed in depth and on a wide front, thus dissipating the power of the enemy artillery. Later waves would profit by passing through gaps, and like those going before them, move swiftly across the danger area. Wherever possible, infantry would actually begin to advance into their own barrage as they went forward. Though counter-intuitive, this principle, 'so successfully taught in the assault battalions, must become general among all infantry. It requires reckless pluck and high morale, as occasional casualties ... must be put up with', but it had the effect of making close fighting with the enemy infantry and machine guns easier.

The attack would normally be led by 'assault detachments', with endeavour made to form these detachments from 'groups of riflemen, which will be reinforced or formed as required'. Whether it was better to employ waves of skirmishers, or waves of assault detachments, or a combination of the two, would be decided on a case-by-case basis. In any event the infantry would be given specific objectives:

> Besides making full use of the weapons at their disposal and exploit- ing the enemy's known weaknesses, the troops must have dash if an assault is to be successful. Success is gained by determined and reckless drive and initiative on the part of every individual man. A check in the attack at one place must not spread to the whole line; infantry which pushes well forward will envelop the parties of the enemy which are standing fast, will sweep them aside and pave the way for the advance of any of their own detachments that are held up. Hesitation leads to failure ... Within the battle sectors the attacks must not be carried out uniformly. Strong points, villages and woods must be neutralised, in certain circumstances by means of smoke clouds. The troops should pass them and, distributed in depth, attack the points which appear likely to offer the least resistance. Rearward waves will capture the strong points etc, by envelopment.

As Hindenburg later observed: 'We were completely renouncing the mass tactics in which the individual soldier finds the driving force in the protection given him by the bodies of men around him'. Indeed such 'protection' had long since been proved illusory. What mattered now was the personal will to do the deed. A set of com- plementary 'Notes' captured in April 1918 stated explicitly: 'Do not attack in dense formations – numbers will not decide, but the use of auxiliary weapons at the right moment'.

Only in small operations would attacking infantry be limited to following precisely laid-down routes. The deeper and more important the attack, the greater the scope for the men on the ground to use their discretion to find their own way, 'provided this action properly conforms to the spirit of the whole operation. In this way, small advantages gained may at once be developed into great successes'. Should assault detachments get bunched up within the enemy defences, the earliest opportunity would be seized to extend into regular skirmish lines, thus avoiding the danger of being surprised in an unsuitable formation.

Machine guns were not just auxiliary weapons for the attacking infantry: they were as much principal weapons as were rifles. With the reduced strengths of most infantry companies in 1918 it was thought that each would be likely to be able to take no more than four light machine guns into the assault. This of course would still be enough for one or more per platoon. Machine gun companies would bring up six heavy machine guns, three more being carried as a reserve. The greatest effort was required to ensure close co-operation between the infantry group and the machine gun allotted to it. Moreover:

> Numerous machine guns must be attached from the very first to the troops leading the assault in order that, where there is a check, they may be available to cover the advance of riflemen and bombers by keeping down the fire from hostile nests, or to repulse hostile counter-attacks. Other machine guns will be at first posted in the neighbourhood of the jumping off position, in readiness to carry out similar tasks.

With a portion of the machine guns going forward with the first line infantry, others were deputed to follow up. This would enable a defence in depth to be mounted upon the captured position, ready to repel any counter-attack.

On occasions, infantry co-ordination with machine gun fire during the attack reached extremes that might have been considered absurd earlier in the war. During one assault in the Wytchaete-Voormezeele area the first battalion of the 13th Reserve Infantry Regiment began by putting sixteen machine guns into action. These 'continually swept the whole of the enemy's position, leaving a gap only four metres wide for the assault'. Far from approaching in any sort of line, or even in small, widely spread assault groups, the entire battalion then advanced using a hedge line for cover. When close enough:

> ... it pushed forward in single file, one assault detachment disposed behind another, and rolled the position up to both flanks, while the machine guns continued to sweep the trenches. The progress made by the assault detachments was signalled to the machine guns by hoisting a helmet. The attack was completely successful.

Significant emphasis was placed on keeping the attack going, indeed, even on allowing the foremost units as much leeway as possible in determining the extent of a penetration:

> In the elan of an attack, good troops often overrun the objective. A quick grasp of the situation often secures successes which would otherwise only be won by renewed preparation. Troops pressing forward, therefore, should not be held too much in hand. In a breakthrough on a large scale, particularly, the boldest decision is always the best.

Where small portions of an assault failed to make headway this was not to be allowed to hold up the entire attack. Rather, troops who had made progress in neighbouring units were to be prepared to assist those flagging portions forward, by giving them support from the flank. Machine guns, light mortars and artillery accompanying the infantry would thus provide immediate 'fire preparation', jump-starting the attack of those who had been stopped.

Though infantry and artillery were seen as the vital 'teeth' arms in *Der Angriff Im Stellungskrieg*, all parts of the army had their roles to play. Cavalry would provide despatch riders and mounted scouts; engineers would undertake preparatory work including mining, help the artillery forward, and support attacks on limited objectives. Signal troops would both set up networks in advance and, in the event of a major breakthrough, establish communications with forward units as quickly as possible. In all events, signallers were to be proactive in the execution of their duty and not assume that making a particular connection was the responsibility of others. Critical was the idea of *Zusammenwirken*, everyone working together, or the 'combining' of efforts for greater effect.

Air forces similarly were to give complete co-operation, whilst not telegraphing the place of the attack by prematurely engaging in frenetic activity over the sector. They were, however, to construct new airfields as clandestinely as possible, complete photographic reconnaissance and help produce maps and sketches of the front. Only when the enemy became obviously aware of the impending onslaught would German air resources be fully committed to 'master the enemy's air forces' – clearing his observation balloons from the sky and shooting down all enemy craft. Bombers would be devoted to deeper penetration, concentrating on 'railway stations, camps, large dumps and aerodromes in turn'. When the enemy attempted to intervene with his own artillery, the German air forces would reply – spotting new battery positions, and then helping friendly infantry forward with ground attacks. The concluding remarks of *Der Angriff Im Stellungskrieg* , signed off by Ludendorff himself, were highly significant:

> The great attack for a breakthrough requires that commanders and troops should free themselves from habits and customs of trench warfare. Methods of warfare and tactics have changed in detail. But the great military principles which formed the backbone of our military training in peace time and to which we owe all great successes in war, are still the old ones. Where they have been forgotten, they must be again aroused.

Whilst the shock tactics of the infantry were undoubtedly a crucial element of the new doctrine, it is dubious whether they could have made much headway without co-ordination with the artillery, as was made clear by *Der Angriff*. The bombardment of 21 March was shattering, as was reported in the memoirs of Herbert Sulzbach, an officer with the 63rd Field Artillery:

> The artillery fire begins at 4.40 a.m., and at 9.40, that is after a five-hour barrage, came the infantry assault and creeping barrage. Meanwhile the evening has come on, and I'm sitting on a limber and can hardly

collect my impressions of today. I'd like to write volumes about this day; it really must be one of the greatest in the history of the world. So the impossible thing has been achieved; the breakthrough has succeeded! The last night of static warfare passed, as I have said above, in the greatest possible excitement after the starting time had been fixed … The darkness begins to lift, very, very slowly; we stand to the guns with our gas masks round our necks, and the time until 4.40 crawls round at a dreadfully slow pace. At last we're there, and with a crash our barrage begins from thousands … of gun barrels and mortars, a barrage that sounds as though the world were coming to an end. For the first hour we only strafe the enemy artillery with alternate shrapnel, Green Cross and Blue Cross [gas shells]. The booming is getting more and more dreadful, especially as we are in a town between the walls of houses … In the middle of this booming I often have to make a break in my fire control duties, since I just can't carry on with all the gas and smoke. The gunners stand in their shirt sleeves, with the sweat running down and dripping off them. Shell after shell is rammed into the breech, salvo after salvo is fired, and you don't need to give fire orders any more, they're in such good spirits, and put up such a good rate of fire, that not a single word of command is needed. In any case, you can now only communicate with the gun teams by using a whistle. At 9.40 the creeping barrage begins, and under its cover the thousands, and thousands more, and tens of thousands of soldiers climb out of the trenches, and the infantry assault begins: and the infantry assault has now succeeded. The limbers come up, and we reach our finest hour when *Leutnant* Knauer gives the order *Nach vorwarts – protzt auf!* 'To the front – limber up!'

Traditionally, most of the credit for the latest artillery tactics has gone to Lieutenant Colonel Georg Bruchmüller – famously dubbed *Durchbruchmüller*, 'Breakthrough-Müller', by Ludendorff. Indeed, Ludendorff penned the text for a monument to the still-living Bruchmüller, erected at Berg Hoheneck, Mittlefranken, in the 1920s, which read:

Oberst G. Bruchmüller Gennant Durchbruchmüller Leitete Am 21 Marz 1918 Die Artillerie Der 18 Armee Deren Fuerwalze Den Grossen Durchruch In Richtung Amiens Ermöglichte.

[Colonel G. Bruchmüller, known as *Durchbruchmüller*, that on the 21 March 1918, led the artillery of the 18th Army 'Fuerwalze' that made possible the great breakthrough in the direction of Amiens.]

At first glance this would appear unequivocal, except for the fact that Ludendorff did not explicitly credit Bruchmüller with new methods, and that the 18th Army was just one of three involved in the opening attacks of the Spring Offensive. What Ludendorff said in his *War Memoirs* of 1919, was:

> As early as July, 1917, he [Bruchmüller] had arranged the employ-ment of the artillery in the breakthrough in East Galicia, and at the time of the attack in March he was Artillery General at the 18th Army Headquarters. His great knowledge and capacity marked him out as one of the most prominent soldiers of this war. His suggestions had already formed the groundwork for the employment of the artillery on 21st March. The artillery of 18th Army was completely imbued with his spirit. This, added to the fact that it struck the weakest point in the enemy's line, contributed to the fine success of that army. The 17th Army, which certainly had the strongest enemy in front of it, worked on similar principles, but the vitalizing energy which emanated from Colonel Bruchmüller was lacking. This is another incidence of the deci-sive influence of personality on the course of war, as in life generally.

What Ludendorff praised in Bruchmüller was not so much inven-tiveness, but drive, organisational skills and man management. As well he might since the *Feuerwalze* had existed since at least mid-1916 and had been used extensively on the Western Front by both sides, as had phased barrages, counter-battery fire, map-predicted fire and – at least in emergencies – fire without pre-registration.

If we look more closely at the events of March 1918, it is also apparent that as well as attacking the weakest enemy, the 18th Army was actually equipped with the strongest artillery: a total of 2,623 guns against 2,234 for the 17th Army, and just 1,751 allo-cated to the 2nd Army. Moreover, the proportion of heavy pieces given to the 18th army was slightly greater than that for the 17th Army. Under such circumstances, it would have been surprising if the 18th Army had not made the best progress; as it was, their performance was only marginally better than that of the 2nd Army, which had the least artillery support. There was also considerable dissension between various officers as to the desirability of some of the innovations which Bruchmüller sought to promote. In this respect, Bruchmüller's key antagonist was General Richard von Berendt, artillery chief of the 17th Army and celebrated pioneer of artillery tactics at Caporetto. Beyond the natural professional jealousies which might arise between two officers who had once been Lieutenants in the same artillery regiment, there were also important matters of detail in disagreement.

Perhaps the most significant of these concerned registration of targets before the main bombardment. The usual procedure was to fire a round or two at the proposed target, and, based on where these fell, corrections could then be made before the main shoot. The most significant argument against this was that the arrival of the registration shots would alert the defenders in the target area, who would either move to another location, or go into deep bunkers. Registration might also spoil the general element of surprise, leading to retaliation in the form of counter-battery or barrage which might do more damage to the would-be attacker than it did to the defender. In certain circumstances, it had therefore been seen as desirable to dispense with the preliminaries and open fire with all guns of a battery on the target merely by determining the range and direction, and setting the angles of elevation and traverse on the guns accordingly. Wildly inaccurate fire could still sometimes be corrected even as the shoot was in progress.

In the improved system promulgated by Bruchmüller, with the support of Ludendorff, fire without registration was known as the 'Pulkowski method'. As Ludendorff explained in his memoirs:

> We had ... to discover some means of dealing with this situation and ensure an adequate effect without ranging. During defensive battles we had already endeavoured to do so without constantly checking the barrage. The errors of the day (due to wind and atmospheric density), as well as the gun errors (due to size of chamber caused by wear, and other changes in the bore and carriage), were permanently determined and allowed for when firing. A system was now most carefully elaborated. The Artillery Meteorological Service was regulated on a

general plan in combination with the General Commanding the Air Forces. In this way the batteries could be informed of the errors of the day with the least possible delay. All guns were tested for errors behind the front. In this way it was possible to determine, by means of simple tables for any gun at any time, how much should be added to, or subtracted from, the normal elevation for any target. It was, of course, a necessary condition that ranges were accurately measured. Faultless maps, trigonometrical and topographical determination of all battery zero points on the ground, and the greatest care in marking targets on the maps, as determined by sound ranging, flash spotting and aerial photography – these were the necessary preliminaries, and enormous work it was. The new procedure was strongly objected to, especially by some of the senior gunners. But it had to be adopted nevertheless and fulfilled all expectations. The training and instruction of the troops in the new method was entrusted to Captain Pulkowsky who carried out his duties with great energy and skill.

In fact, the basic idea was anything but new. As early as the seventeenth century, gunners such as Englishman William Eldred and others had encouraged the production of gun-specific fire tables to improve accuracy. During 1917, fire without registration had been discussed by the Royal Artillery, but not widely used, being seen as risky. Again, what was notable with Bruchmüller was the application of method to a specific circumstance and the combination of various more or less novel techniques to produce a coherent doctrine. Yet the pertinence of the 'Pulkowski method' to the circumstances of March 1918 was still much debated. Amongst other things, Berendt and his colleagues argued – perhaps correctly – that in the conditions of the Western Front, pre-registration was not such a big handicap as Bruchmüller and his well-placed confederates supposed. Whilst trench garrisons could run away, or go deep, fortifications and batteries would not so easily escape, and in fact, places that were abandoned straight away were effectively neutralised on the cheap. Moreover, in an environment which had experienced shelling – organised, random, 'ritualised' and otherwise – over a period of years, the arrival of a small number of extra projectiles might well escape notice. Registration could also be effectively disguised by the shooting of other missions, real or dummy, at the same time. In short, Eastern and Western Front conditions were different, and the old tactical tenet of making theory fit circumstance, rather than bending reality to fit a theory, held good.

If the foregoing concerning traditional registration was controversial, there was definitely much in Bruchmüller's methods of 1918 which had been used before – if in a less systematic way. Creeping barrages, or *Feuerwalze*, had been known about for a long time. Arguably, the prototype was the 'lifting' barrage, moving from target to target, which was in use during late 1915. Bruchmüller was certainly experimenting with such concepts about this time on the Eastern Front. Creeping barrages proper were developed during 1916, with one claimant to first use of the perfected technique being the British at Montauban on 1 July, though all parties, including the French, had incorporated the idea by September.

Short barrages, or 'Hurricane Bombardments', which limited the reaction time available to enemy reserves and took advantage of the short-term stunning effect of shelling, were also long in gestation. A number occurred preparatory to 1915 attacks, though probably as much because supplies of munitions were limited as through any theoretical consideration of their superiority. Bruchmüller used four- and five-hour preparation periods in the East on a fairly regular basis in both 1915 and 1916. Field Marshal von Hindenburg remarked in his memoirs that the French used the idea during the reconquest of the battlefield of Verdun in late 1916, and that their version of it took him by surprise:

> For this attack the French commander had abandoned the former practice of an artillery preparation extending over days or weeks. By increasing the rate of fire of the artillery and trench mortars to the extreme limit of capacity of material and men, only a short period of preparation had preceded the attack, which had then been launched immediately against the physically exhausted and morally shaken defenders. We already had experience of this method of enemy preparation for the attack in the course of the long attrition battles, but as the herald to a great infantry attack it was a novelty to us, and it was perhaps just this feature which doubtless produced so important a success. Taking it all round, on this occasion the enemy hoisted us with our own petard.

Perhaps the Entente powers were slower to refine the short bombardment, but by 1917 had grasped its utility, and used it many times with success. After March 1918 it was standard practice for the British, with the French issuing a directive to similar effect on 12 July. Having built up equipment and expertise on the French model, the Americans also adopted short bombardments in September. The use of light artillery to accompany attacking infantry had been experimented with for at least a couple of hundred years. In the Great War context it was pioneered by the Germans, but also known to the French at an early stage, and had been used by the Austrians. It was not developed to any extent by the British, who put their faith in tanks as being superior in this role.

Post-war, Bruchmüller would reinforce his reputation with the publication of a number of writings, including the 1921 book *Die Deutschen Artillerie in Durchbruchschlachten*, but his old critics were far from silenced. *Major* General Hans Waechter, for example, blamed Bruchmüller for the failure of the Champagne-Marne offensive later in 1918, because he was rigid and dogmatic. What had been novel the first time became entirely predictable the fifth time it was used. Nevertheless, Generals Bernhardi and von Kuhl both spoke up in Bruchmüller's defence, at least partly on the grounds that it was difficult to see what other methods might have been applied. Perhaps most worryingly for the Bruchmüller camp, one of the critics was none other than Hermann Geyer, the man credited with *Der Angriff Im Stellungskrieg* – the new tactical bible. In 1935, when Geyer had himself risen to the rank of Lieutenant General, he submitted a piece to the *Militar-Wochenblatt* in which he suggested that the key figure in obtaining acceptance for the Pulkowski method was actually his old colleague Colonel Max Bauer. The editor buried this divisive story, perhaps as much for the sake of unity and the good of the army as through any concern for historical accuracy. Bruchmüller indubitably deserves his place in the pantheon; yet to say that he represented the future, whilst his contemporaries represented the past, is at best simplistic. It is also true that in certain technical respects the spring offensive fell short of Ludendorff's own expectations. The key faults lay primarily with diplomacy and strategy, for which Ludendorff himself must carry a fair proportion of the burden. Yet the much-lauded tactics themselves had their inbuilt problems: running out of control was one, but there were others.

If the latest version of *Stoss*, or shock, tactics was brilliant in breaking through defended positions, the human cost of doing so was greater than ever. Whilst serious casualties were certainly inflicted, the Germans themselves were now losing men at an unsustainable rate. On 21 March best estimates were that about 11,000 Germans died, 29,000 were wounded and a few hundred were taken prisoner. By mid-April the losses of all categories had escalated to about 250,000. Repeated attacks over the next two to three months added at least another 100,000. There was much to the argument that by winning so much the German army was rapidly enervating itself to the point of impotence, whilst Allied losses were continually replaced. Local tactical victories were not reaping bigger dividends, and simply gaining ground did very little to finish the enemy. Too late, the Germans resumed the defensive, and in 'black' August a further 225,000 troops were lost; alarmingly higher proportions were being captured or going missing than had been the case just six months before. Hungry and exhausted men, and new recruits, were now less worried by the prospect of captivity. By the time collecting numbers had become futile, just before the Armistice, the yearly total lost to one cause or another had reached approximately a million, of whom something over 300,000 were dead – the largest single year total on the Western Front during the war. Hindenburg would be moved to pejoratively describe the German army of late 1918 as more 'a militia' than a properly fit and trained fighting force.

As ever, artillery cut huge holes in infantry attacking in the open, and even if less dense formations moderated the impact, artillery itself had improved in response. Even during the onslaught of 21 March by no means all were protected by surprise and the elements. As a Captain of the 53rd Infantry Regiment, already acting as battalion commander through lack of officers, recorded:

> I had just left my dug out and had gone 50 metres and was passing behind the 6th Company when an English shell landed two metres away in the last squad of the 6th. At first I was thrown to the ground, and when I jumped up again and came forwards there was none to be seen but the dead and a wounded *Gefreiter* of the 6th. I grabbed

him under the arm and ran with him towards the front as fast as I could. After a little while I resumed connection with the unit, but of my staff one *Leutnant* was dead, the Adjutant badly wounded, and the Pioneer officer wounded, of ten orderlies by that evening only one was left with me. The others were dead or wounded. Only a miracle left me untouched, but so bespattered with the blood of others that it was generally assumed that I was wounded ... The 6th Company could no longer be found.

If the German techniques of March 1918 were in many ways similar to those used at Cambrai a few months earlier, and the Allies (especially the British) were already working on similar – if less bold and reckless – lines, with the crucial addition of large numbers of tanks, it takes considerable explaining why the Spring Offensive came to be regarded as such a significant tactical watershed. Perhaps the most important reason that the 1918 offensive was thought of as new and different was that since Verdun almost two years earlier, there had been no major German assault in the west. Almost all the attacking that the Kaiser's armies had done in that time had been in the east; with attacks in the west kept on a relatively small scale as 'restorative' counter-attacks, for example, on the Somme or at Cambrai. Another, more prosaic, reason for the initial success and psychological impact of the *Kaiserschlact* was that, for once, the German forces had actually managed to achieve a significant local superiority in numbers. With the October Revolution and the Russian collapse in the autumn of 1917, it suddenly became possible to transfer large numbers of German troops from the Eastern front to the West. The fight had to be brief and conclusive, for as Hindenburg later observed in his memoirs: 'we had neither the resources, nor the time [for a] battle of material'.

By March 1918 the bulk of the available German forces, about three-quarters of a million men, were in the area of the selected *Schwerpunkt*, opposite the British 5th and 3rd Army sectors. All in all, the Germans mustered approximately 76 divisions along this front, against 29 found by the British. More than 50 German divisions would play a part in the assault of 21 March, falling on 20 of those of the British defenders – a figure very close to the three-to-one superiority sometimes regarded as the viability level for a successful attack against prepared positions in modern wars. Both sides would in fact feed more divisions into the fight, the early British and French reinforcements being outnumbered by those the Germans had to hand. Unlike the appalling weather the British and Canadians had faced at the Third Ypres the previous autumn, the elements were at first kind to the Kaiser's armies. In contrast with the deep mud of Flanders, the going was relatively good: natural fog supplemented the man-made efforts of gas and smoke in shrouding the first advance. Naturally, there was some variation across the battlefield, but near rivers and still pools the atmosphere was so thick that the attackers presented no target at all. *Major* Hartwig Pohlmann with 36th Division remembered that at one point he actually had to tell his men to grasp the belts of their comrades, so as not to become lost in the fog.

General Sir Hubert Gough, commander of the British Fifth Army, who was relieved of his post on 28 March and sent home a week later in the wake of the opening of the offensive, certainly felt aggrieved that the disadvantages with which he was faced had not been taken into account. As he wrote in his *Fifth Army* of 1931:

> No definite orders about the future of the Fifth Army were at first given to its staff, but by the end of November [1917] we were able to make a good guess that our destination was the French front on the right of the Third Army. Up to that date this had been a quiet sector and was lightly held by two French corps only: but though quiet at the moment, it was a considerable addition to the British front – about 28 miles – to which Haig very naturally objected and against which he strongly protested.
>
> The French argument was that the share of the front to be held by them and the British should be calculated principally on the mileage of the total front. Strategical reasons were not considered; the vital importance of the Channel Ports to Great Britain in general and the British Army in particular was overlooked, and the strength of the German Army opposite the British as compared to its strength on the French front received little or no consideration: nor did the fact that serious fighting was impossible on more than half of the front of the French Army – in the semi-mountainous country of the Vosges, behind which lay great fortresses.

Our mission at French GQG, however, strongly espoused the French view, and Lloyd George and his cabinet having more confidence in the French Command than in Haig, the latter's protests were over-ridden and we eventually had to take over the whole of this great increase in front. The results which quickly followed placed the British Army in the greatest peril, at the same time thoroughly shaking the confidence and nerve of the Cabinet at home when it awoke by the end of March to the full consequences of its own decision.

Although the merits and demerits of Gough's generalship may continue to be debated, there can be little doubt that he himself helped to encourage the idea of von Hutier as a maverick tactical genius and bogeyman. Gough records that early in 1918 he was provided with a pamphlet by the French staff which described the enemy preparations 'for the battles of Riga and Caporetto', and that he quickly perceived similarities between the situations described and the current position on the Fifth Army front:

> I had just learned that von Hutier had appeared opposite us in command of the German Eighteenth Army. Except for a short period in command of a Guard Division in France in 1914, his service had been continuously on the Russian front, where he had been responsible for many large-scale and highly successful attacks. The fact of his presence now on my front seemed to portend that something of a similar nature to those battles was to be attempted.

A report on the situation was indeed penned by Gough to GHQ on 1 February, in which he noted not only von Hutier's presence, but some of the more obvious difficulties that Fifth Army might face in the event of a major enemy offensive. Perhaps the most important paragraph in this document was the fourth, in which he pointed out that the most recent German attacks 'have been characterised by a short bombardment up to about six hours and the most strenuous efforts to obtain surprise. These efforts I cannot be sure of defeating'. In the Gough account, Riga and von Hutier were the keys.

Of course, retrospectively, Gough had an interest in building up the reputation and importance of von Hutier: for the more omnipotent the opponent appeared, the more excusably his own performance could be interpreted. Moreover, Gough also argued that his instructions from Haig, given during February 1918, specifically allowed him to give ground, should the need arise. He was told that the forward zones did not protect anything vital enough:

> ... to warrant reinforcements being thrown into the fight, counter-attacks on a large scale being launched, or the battle being fought out in the Battle Zone, unless the general situation at the time makes such a course advisable. It may well be desirable to fall back on the rearward defences of Peronne and the Somme while linking up with the Third Army in the north, and preparing for counter-attack.

Of course, the British went back a lot further than this contingency suggested; nevertheless, Gough had an important point. Like the Germans, the British were now thinking more flexibly, to the extent that repeatedly fighting over the same trench lines, to no definite advantage, was now regarded as unnecessary. Giving ground in a fighting retreat might, in the long term, inflict more damage on the party that took the battlefield. Sadly for Gough, no one had thought it worthwhile to impress these strategic and tactical niceties upon the cabinet, and any sacrifice of soil was bound to go down badly with the French.

If Gough felt constrained to defend with inadequate resources, it is almost equally true that the Germans felt bound to attack. The Spring of 1918 offered what was all too small a window of opportunity. Only for a few months could the German army count on the local numerical advantage over Britain or France it had gained by the exit of Russia from the war. If they waited too long the numbers of Americans would tip the statistical odds again. To do nothing was to sit and invite the inevitable: blockade was slowly strangling the German economy, and eventually the war would be lost even if there was no more actual fighting. On the German home front, food prices had tripled since 1914, and wages failed to keep up even though more money was in circulation. Munitions producers did quite well; most others did not. The winter of 1916 to 1917 had already been dubbed the 'Turnip Winter' because there was little else to eat, potato crops being greatly reduced. A curious exhibition mounted at Charlottenburg featured no less than ninety ways to prepare the turnip. As Richard Hoffman complained in his book *Frontsoldaten*, progressively everything was being made of home-produced substitutes. 'The entire homeland was *ersatz! Ersatz* Battalions, *ersatz* butter, *ersatz* eggs, *ersatz* coffee, *ersatz* sugar, *ersatz* shirts, *ersatz* men … The only thing that was still stable was the front'. Bread was no longer purely a matter of wheat and rye: the euphemistically named *K-Brot*, or 'war bread', contained potato, other ground vegetables and similar ingredients. Soldiers' narratives speak of tins of dubious substitutes, probably extracted from fish, and dried vegetables that could, with only a modicum of exaggeration, be described as *Stacheldraht* , or 'barbed wire'. Bizarrely, tinned 'bully beef', of which most British soldiers were heartily sick, became a delicacy for their German opposite numbers, who were keen to capture it during raids.

Operation Michael in March 1918 was just the first phase of a much bigger plan, and Ludendorff was not about to stop midway through what had been billed as an 'offensive for peace'. However, he was in something of a quandary: whether he should stick to the blue print for attack as originally formulated, or act on the opportunity of the moment to press the issue where the greatest success had already been achieved. As he himself would attempt to justify his crucial decisions in 'The Two Battles of the Marne':

I was now faced with the difficult problem of deciding whether I should stop the victorious progress of General von Hutier's Eighteenth Army, which had been entrusted to cover our left flank against the French. This would mean forcing a decision on our right wing north of the Somme. It would necessitate throwing more effectives into battle, so as to overcome unexpected stubborn opposition of the enemy at the other point. The alternative was an inauguration of an entirely new strategical plan. When a commander is bent on breaking through the enemy's positions it is not always possible to adhere closely to a preconceived plan, for the break does not always occur where it is most confidently expected. The strategist who sticks to his initial plan when things do not develop as he expected is in danger of losing his objective. To break through an enemy's line effectively, it is necessary to exploit any initial success at any weak point. The gap thus forced must be widened as a flood widens a hole in a wall …

So it was that the battle now developed on the German left wing with 17th Army heading in the direction of Doullens, with the objective of driving a great wedge between the British and French. Though fully in keeping with German thinking as expressed in *The Attack in Position Warfare* it was a fateful and controversial decision, and one which would later be criticised in the German Official History. Ludendorff's offensive had achieved great things, but by failing to focus on the original target until it was completely destroyed, and being unable to rest his really battle-worthy troops of the 'attack' divisions, there was a growing danger of squandering an advantage which had cost so much to win. In April the attack was turned against the British again, this time with 50 divisions in Flanders. Haig actually used the phrase 'backs to the wall' in a 'Special Order to the British Army in France and Flanders'. Yet the further forward the German army struggled, the more difficult became its lines of supply. Moreover, the striking of desperate blows, by a finite force against disparate targets, served to mitigate their cumulative impact.

However much the minor tactics had improved, many German soldiers had a very similar experience to the French and British – who had for so long been attacking in the opposite direction. Just such a one was Marine Herbert Schroeter:

> At 8 a.m. we started. After a few hundred metres, when we crossed a road that led to Amiens, we were met by a terrific explosion of machine gun fire. In the middle of the road I was hit by a machine-gun bullet which shattered my left upper arm. Both my legs were also hit slightly, just below the knees. Next to me my good friend Ludwig Krause was shot dead with a gaping wound to his chest. The other comrades of my *Gruppe* stormed forward and, as I found out later, all of them fell before they reached the English position. I crawled into a deep furrow at the side of the road, seeking cover from the continuous machine gun fire. I thought I was going to bleed to death …

Ernst Jünger, whose experience of the 'Great Offensive' had begun promisingly enough in the 'white heat of recklessness', with an advance so significant he could not believe it was true, was now also mired in gore and enemy counter-attacks.

A man of the 76th, close to me, shot off cartridge after cartridge, looking perfectly wild and without thought of cover, till he collapsed in
streams of blood. A shot had smashed his forehead with a report
like a breaking board. He doubled up in his corner of the trench, and
there he remained in a crouching attitude, his head leaning against
the side. His blood poured on to the ground as though poured out
of a bucket. The snorting death rattles sounded at longer intervals
and at last ceased. I seized his rifle and went on firing ... We tried
several times to work our way forward by crawling flattened out
over the bodies of the Highlanders across the undug part, but we
were driven back each time by machine gun fire and rifle grenades.
Every casualty I saw was a fatal one. In this way the forward part
of our trench was filled with dead; and in turn we were constantly
reinforced from the rear. Soon there was a light or a heavy machine
gun at every traverse. I stood behind one of these 'lead squirts' and
shot till my forefinger was blackened with smoke. When the cool-
ing water had evaporated, the tins were handed round and to the
accompaniment of not very polite jokes and by a very simple expedient filled up again.

Such was the sort of war that artist-soldier Otto Dix would later
describe as 'reducing mankind to the state of beasts, with its hun-
ger, vermin, mud and insane noises'.

So it was that Operation Michael would be followed by Operation
Georgette and Operation Blücher. All three gained some ground,
but none of them succeeded in shattering the Allied armies beyond
redemption, and with each successive stroke the offensive power
of the German army ebbed. Georgette was a relatively inconclusive
fight against the British. In May Blücher swept towards the Marne
river against the French, but stalled. Operation Marneschütz-
Reims, a last gasp in July, got a short distance across the Marne
using every available ounce of strength. Thereafter, defence against
Allied attacks would not be so easy. The German position was over-
extended, well beyond the old and devastated battlefields of 1916
and 1917. Trenches and defended positions had to be dug again,
and there would not be time to recreate the deep zones that existed
in Flanders and on the Somme. As Roger Chickering has summa-
rised in his book *Imperial Germany and the Great War*:

Ludendorff's last offensive failed to win the war for Germany. It also fatally undermined the capacities of his armies to defend themselves in the positions to which they had advanced – at a time when allied forces were at last accumulating the advantage that had eluded Ludendorff.

After mid 1918 neither a successful long-term defence nor another major attack appeared possible. The British were already planning offensives for 1919, and Allied industry carried on producing war materials apace – an Anglo-American 'Liberty' tank was just one of the new devices to be expected. As Hindenburg wearily observed, without being able to mount an attack, a 'slow death from exhaustion' would be the German fate. But either way it was soon to end. The popular patriotic call now sounded a valid prophesy:

Wir haben alle nur einen Willen Siegen oder Sterben!
We all have only one desire, Victory or Death!

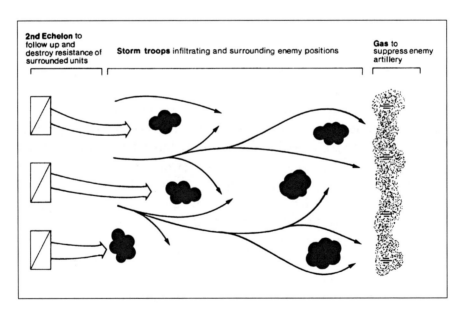

German offensive technique. (Image courtesy of Paddy Griffith/Antony Bird Publications)

Conclusion

Der Sturm brach ein in Deutsches Land…
Nehmt kaltes Eisen in die hand!
An Weichsel, Rhein und See und Sund
Schlag, Tambour, Schlag den Wirbel rund!
Und sollt' die Welt voll Teufel sein,
Deutsch Eisen trägt den Tod hinein

The storm breaks in on German land…
Take cold steel in your hand!
On Vistula, Rhine, sea and Baltic sound
Beat drum, and whip the whirlwind round!
And should the world be full of evil,
German metal strikes it dead.

Sturmlied ('The Storm Song'), 1914.
From a copy of *Deutsche Kriegsklange*, Volume One, used by Bavarian
Landwehr Infantry Regiment Nr 2, 1916.

The period 1914 to 1918 undoubtedly saw vast changes in battle-field tactics. This was partly a matter of technological advance, with the inventions of the tank, chemical warfare, the light machine gun, the flame-thrower and fighter and bomber aircraft – to name only the most obvious. The tactical advance was also a function of reinvention and production: grenades, artillery, trenches, machine guns, armour, barbed wire and a dozen other technical marvels had all existed before 1914, but all were vastly improved, or manufactured on incredible scales, and often both. As Von der Goltz had prophesied, both sides had directed all their 'moral energy' into a life and death struggle, and the sum of the combatants' intelligence had been employed for 'mutual destruction'. We should not, however, overlook the human factor. New weapons needed new military structures, new tactical units, new training and education. Individual pioneers, trainers and theoreticians made sure that the increase in killing power was not just used in the same old way, but fitted to circumstance and purpose. Sometimes two novelties used in conjunction proved far more effective than either one alone, or both used sequentially. Sometimes the tactical possibilities were missed for a while, then dramatically exploited. This ferment of innovation is too often forgotten when we see how trivial the geographic advances were for much of the war on the Western Front, or we are overwhelmed by the horror of casualty statistics and fighting conditions, which so far exceeded anything previously encountered.

At its most basic human level, the war saw a huge change in the way infantry units fought. In the German instance, soldiers of the infantry battalions in 1914 had been identically armed, and acted according to a uniform set of regulations, even if this template was sometimes breached in detail. Advances were made in various forms of column, but, when close enough to the enemy, most of the fighting had been done in skirmish lines. The lines advanced by portions, often platoons, executing short rushes before going prone to shoot. A charge finished off the enemy and occupied his position. Though NCOs had a role to play, most minor tactical decisions were made by officers. A company of six machine guns within the infantry regiment could provide supporting fire, but the weapon of the period was not suited to moving up rapidly with the forefront of the attack, as it was heavy and required setting up.

By 1918 all this had altered. Platoons and squads were now viable tactical entities in their own right. With squads fighting scattered on the battlefield, tactical decisions were regularly required at the micro level. NCOs had to take many decisions, and instances when the ordinary soldiers – as for example isolated machine gunners – had to determine their own course of action were not infrequent. As Ludendorff observed:

It was necessary to instruct the troops according to the tactical lessons learned in the latest fighting. These were, more extended formations for infantry, greater importance attached to storm troop tactics, better co-operation between *Gruppe* and companion arms, and between infantry and artillery ... On all occasions I emphasised the need of not forgetting the necessary formation for defence, and of recognising the moment when the attack must be stopped and the defence resumed.

After the war, the idea of the squad that could be tactically self-sufficient would become the universal norm. The MG 08/15 continued to be the cornerstone of the German *Gruppe* but was supplanted by the air-cooled MG 13 in the early 1930s, and this itself was eventually replaced by the MG 34, an outstanding, truly 'general purpose' machine gun. Though squad sizes varied, and weapon technology moved on, the concept of a machine gun providing tactical support to a group of riflemen has remained a constant right up to the present day. This was not just true of the Germans but also of other nations: the British, for example, who only replaced their Lewis guns with Bren guns in the late 1930s, and the Americans, who retained their original Browning Automatic Rifle or 'BAR' right through the Korean War.

'Revolution' is an overused and often inexact term, but the idea that there was a revolution in infantry tactics during the First World War is persuasive. From the early Renaissance onward, military writers and generals had rediscovered classical ideas regarding close battlefield formations and applied them ever more exactly to their own times. Pikes had 'worked' as a weapon of war because they were used by closely formed troops; firearms likewise had become battle-winning weapons because they were grouped and used according to systematic drills. Individual fighters became progressively less significant with passing decades. Dense bodies of men, or shoulder-to-shoulder lines, were the picture of virtually every battlefield from about 1450 to 1850. In European warfare, barrack yards and drill manuals became the norm. The drive was towards standardisation in all things: standardised formations, standardised uniforms, standardised weapons, standardised munitions, standardised food. During the Industrial Revolution, the dream of standardisation had gradually become a reality. The advent of skirmishers armed with firearms, the invention of the rifle and more efficient artillery had begun to add some diversity to this picture during the seventeenth century, but those who fought in loose bands were in a minority most commonly to be seen in broken terrain. Successively, the American Civil War, Franco-Prussian, Boer War and Russo-Japanese War shook the orthodox tyranny of lines and columns, but they had not broken it. Only during 1914 to 1918 was it fully and finally admitted that dressed lines and fire by volley had no place in modern war. The plethora of new inventions, and a dawning realisation of the significance of camouflage, both hastened this change and underlined it.

For ordinary soldiers the change from large bodies of men to small, from the highly visible to the invisible and 'the empty battlefield', was much more than a technical curiosity. Three of the major impacts on the infantryman were particularly important. The first was that he had to take on a more technical job. No longer did he handle just one weapon, according to one drill, which could be learnt entirely mechanically; now he would have to master at least two, and very probably more, grenades and machine weapons being only the most obvious. Drills were useful in some circumstances (such as a gas attack) but now the ability to think for oneself, to take cover, shoot, and move independently was more and more vital. Literacy became increasingly useful in such an environment. The second important change was that the ordinary soldier was no longer under the ever-watchful eye of an officer all the while that he performed his duty. Individual *Gruppe*, lone snipers, machine gun teams and sentries very often had to take their own decisions: to shoot or not to shoot; to stand and fight or to run. This could be a significant and onerous responsibility. The third change stems from the second: since officers were less apparent to the rank and file, non-commissioned officers had to take far more of the burden of command, no longer simply relay everything from above and making sure that orders were obeyed. In the German instance, *Gruppe* and *Zuge* might well operate under the direction of NCOs for long periods. The basic framework might be part of company orders, but how these directions were carried out would probably be decided on the spot by a man of the labouring classes with only a piece of lace or a button on his collar to distinguish him from his fellows. Such people needed to inspire great trust or great fear, or possibly both. The commanding officer might be the 'father' of a unit, but the top NCO was its 'mother'.

Various authorities, most importantly Bruce Gudmundsson and Martin Samuels, have claimed that the Germans led the way in the development of tactics during the First World War. Contrary voices have suggested that in fact this accolade should belong to the British or French. In reality, the picture was fogged, for as Clausewitz once observed, 'war consists of a continuous interaction of opposites'. Not only did different armies achieve leads at different times, but within each army there were tactical strengths and weaknesses that varied over the course of the war. Often it was the availability, or lack, of a weapon that helped to dictate which side gained the upper hand; sometimes it was quirks of organisation or tradition, or the presence or lack of a champion for a particular method. Circumstance could critically alter who appeared to be winning the tactical and technological race. When one side was attacking it mattered little how advanced their defensive methods might be. When another was defending, their degree of advance in the art of the attack was untried, and for that matter not obvious to the researcher. The productivity or faults of different attacking methods were often apparent to the defender, who might take note of enemy tactics for his own purposes.

Contrary to much of what has been published, relatively little of what was new was developed on the Eastern Front: most came from the West. This should not surprise us. This is where the majority of the Germans were, where the majority of the Reich Marks were spent, where the majority of the shells were fired and where the most industrially advanced enemies were encountered. On the eastern side of Germany, the front stretched over 600 miles of predominantly flat terrain through Poland, and then on again along the Hungarian border. Deep defences were difficult to establish here, and proved far more brittle than in the West – manoeuvre was never quite dead. Though little of the new tactics were developed in the East, the Russians struggled from an early stage – particularly in terms of production, distribution, training and communication. German sophistication was therefore most marked, apparently, when set against the armies of the Czar.

Germany certainly achieved overall early leads in sniping, grenade fighting, trench mortars and flame-throwers. Some inkling that super-heavy artillery, machine guns, trench mortars and grenades might be of significance in a future conflict had been realised by the command as early as 1905. Germany also developed highly effective defensive tactics, especially in the middle war period, and particularly with the use of reinforced concrete. She failed to produce light machine guns quickly enough, and perhaps critically was a dismal failure when it came to the tank – a story of far too little too late. An early lead in gas turned to a deficit towards the end of the war. She led the world with anti-tank rifles and sub machine guns, but these advantages counted for little at the time they were achieved. In the important field of artillery technology and tactics, the race was close, and different micro battles were won by both sides. German heavy artillery achieved a vital lead and huge technological sophistication with the Paris guns of 1918, but creeping barrages and hurricane bombardments were adopted by increments in different places at different times. The Allies may have been slower on average, but universal adoption of such things was not achieved by the Germans much more quickly. Bruchmüller was no myth, but his ideas were ahead only by a nose – and not in all spheres of artillery operations at that.

That both sides gleaned much of what they knew from each other is clear from German, British, French and American tactical manuals and training literature. There are often directly translated quotes and sometimes references to specific enemy actions from which a lesson has been learned. In his book *The Poisonous Cloud*, L.F. Haber coined the phrase 'involuntary cross fertilisation' for this phenomena, but it was 'involuntary' only from the perspective of the side whose techniques were being copied, and often bettered, by the other. The process was in fact a testament to the successes of military intelligence, and the officers of the fighting arms and staff alike, who recognised what was of value on the other side of the line. A common lexicon of war already existed amongst military men in 1914, and paradoxically, the more they fought each other, the more similar they became. In 1917 the German General Staff's 'Intelligence Section' was actually renamed as the *Fremde Heere*, 'foreign armies', section. Its duties included not just obvious matters

concerning strategy but the gathering of information on organisation, new formations and *taktischer Massnahmen,* 'tactical measures'.
Other countries did very similar things. As in previous centuries
of conflict, the general direction of movement between enemies
locked in a protracted struggle was towards common methods
– the things that worked – with the useless or decorative falling
by the wayside. In what many German writers would later openly
acknowledge as a Darwinian struggle, what was 'different' was
either proved successful and became the norm, or was promptly
abandoned altogether. Many, on all sides, spoke of the industriali-
sation of the war, the end of glory, and of growing 'mechanisation'.
For the Germans, who gradually lost the struggle of materials and
manpower, there was an increasing tendency to see the battlefield
as one of human quality (their own) against the inhumanity of mass
and the machine (that of the enemy). Comparing Germans and
Britons, economist Werner Sombart was inclined to see the struggle
as a matter of 'heroes' against 'traders'.

In the specific terms of small-unit tactics, it was certainly true
that by the latter stages of the war the similarities between the
various nations fighting on the Western Front were greater than
the differences. In British, American, French and German infantry
tactics alike, there was now a growing emphasis on small groups
with their own support, and the British and French had also taken
at least some of the pioneering steps. As early as the latter part of
the Battle of the Somme, German observers were noting that while
the larger British attacks were often still unimaginative, smaller
sub-units such as machine gun crews, bombing parties and patrols
were trained in 'independent action'. Similar remarks were made
about the French during their retaking of the Verdun battlefield.

However, German methods were different in a number of ways.
Perhaps from the perspective of the Allied powers, immersed in an
erroneous belief that Prussian troops were still automatons from the
eighteenth century, drilled by the lash and by rote into unthinking
obedience, it came as an unpleasant surprise to learn the importance
of *Auftrag* (mission-led) tactics and 'directive command'. Far from
being completely prescriptive, German orders to troops were often
based on the sensible premise that there was a task to be achieved,
but the method by which this was accomplished was open to

latitude on the part of the subordinate. What mattered ultimately was not that the detail was followed, but that the job was done. As the history of *Reserve Infanterie Regiment Nr 86* pointed out:

> On our side the leaders never cease to impress the men that whatever orders and instructions might be given, they will prove inadequate in the event of anything serious, for the situation will change from one moment to the next. Success might open an opportunity which must be exploited without loss of time, while somewhere else a situation might develop which demands a change of plan. Thus our officers and men develop as independent strategists. They work within the broad concept of orders and guidelines, but the decisive action is often the work of officers – and men as well – who are acting on their own authority. The passing chance would have been a matter of history if they had tried to seek the approval of higher circles.

This turned out to be particularly valuable both in the context of the trench war, and of the attack, during the period 1915 to 1918. In defensive battles, shelling and repeated enemy assaults meant that small bodies of troops might be cut off for days. During rapid advances, troops often outran their communications. In such circumstances junior leaders who were trained and expected to perform with self reliance were at a premium, and such concepts added much to the resilience and performance of the German army in both defence and attack.

Yet there were mechanistic reasons as to how a flexible *modus operandi* came to be more likely in the context of the German military system. For the first part, German generals could assume that many of their men, whenever they were called to the colours, were already soldiers with basic training. Long-standing conscription and a system of reserves, which carried on liabilities of duty until a man was forty-five, meant that the rudiments could usually be assumed. In 1914 there were *Landsturm* and *Landwehr* men, and many NCOs, who had learned their trade with the active army years before and been kept in some sort of useful condition by periodic training. Many German soldiers had long since learned the basics of the trade, and so were ready to be taught new ideas sooner than citizens coming to the forces afresh. The idea of conscription being used to form a pool of manpower ready to rejoin the colours went back to the days of Scharnhorst and the Prussian Wars of Liberation, and also chimed in with the even older concept of military service as being at the core of the Prussian state. What outsiders saw as 'militarism', many Germans therefore regarded as a sensible inbuilt survival system, and indeed the mainspring of the very existence of the German Empire. In practice, this meant that even quite late in the war a high proportion of the army had pre-war soldiering experience. The Great War historian Martin Middlebrook has suggested that in 1918 one third to one half of the average German platoon were pre-war soldiers, whilst just one or two men in a similar British unit could boast such experience. The figures may be inexact, but the general principle of the argument is correct.

Germany was young, and for much of its existence it had been common sense – even necessary – for senior commanders not to attempt to be too proscriptive about detail. Individual states had their own sensibilities; their own ways of doing things; their own regiments and uniforms; their own Royal houses and decorations. In the cases of Bavaria, Saxony and Wurttemberg, they even had their own war ministries. Whilst these were gradually being assimilated, it remained politic, and more productive, to concentrate on the tasks in hand; in short, what Germans had in common, not on what divided them. German training and German war plans alike emerged from a world picture of being outnumbered, encircled and threatened with division by others. Force had often been used successfully in the past as the pragmatic solution – though not in the new age of quick-firing artillery and machine guns. The maxims of Clausewitz and his *Vom Kriege* undoubtedly remained important. War could be a continuation of policy; the moral element was crucial; determination and intelligence were key qualities in a leader – but one could only learn about war from either being in one, or studying those past.

Waiting and doing nothing was commonly accounted a cardinal military sin. Both training and planning therefore stressed the radical and aggressive answer to military problems. The role models (Frederick the Great, Blücher, Moltke the elder, Bismarck, and a dozen others) had achieved by action, not by inaction. Having to trust subordinates to do things became a fact of life. The German army was not replete with large numbers of officers relative to the numbers of men, and as the war progressed, there was less inclination than in the old democracies to throw open this privilege to wider sections of society. A high proportion of commanders died. Luckily, the German educational system was a good one, and NCOs were often able to fulfil roles which other countries might have regarded as requiring the input of officers. This may well have helped when it came to the question of investing ever smaller units with decision making.

Perhaps the most extreme contrast was with Britain. The British Army ethos came from a very different direction: it was formed in a world where it was Britannia that ruled the waves and the Navy was the 'Senior Service'. If the army succeeded in surviving, the Navy would eventually succeed in degrading the enemy's will to resist beyond the point of no return. The numbers who died of starvation are unclear, but the blockade of Germany definitely denied overseas trade, and gradually ground down the opposition through shortage and eventually malnutrition. More positively, the British military ideal came from a fear of too much military power. No Hindenburg or Ludendorff would arise to assume quasi-dictatorial power. Politically, there was already an idea afoot that for elected politicians, other peoples' money was a good deal cheaper than voters' blood. The big attacks that the British army made during the first three years of war were mainly at the behest of others: to help reduce pressure on Russia, to distract from Verdun and to take the burden from the French in 1917. Rarely did British Generals or politicians take any unilateral decision to go on the offensive. Though huge sacrifices were ultimately made, British leaders were initially reluctant to fight a general European war, and certainly fearful of having to put vast numbers of 'ordinary men' on the battlefield. A major world Empire had to be guarded by a few, and, to be practical, a modest army strength had to be offset by a modicum of consent on behalf of the ruled. Units were spread very thinly across a globe with poor and relatively slow communication. In such a situation the radical answer was often the wrong one, and rarely was it possible to bring together large bodies of troops for training. Conscription was regarded with great suspicion. Not for nothing did German observers often look at the British as a ridiculously small army, composed essentially of otherwise unemployable professionals, led by a somewhat ridiculous caste of 'sporting gentlemen' in uniforms like golfing suits.

Though British and German army methods were in fact more similar than many experts like to admit, arguably the key philosophical difference was ultimately over the fine balancing point between initiative and recklessness, and tactics appeared to fit the strategy. For Germany in the summer of 1914, in Russia in 1915, at Verdun in 1916 and again in 1918, time was probably a greater issue than any one of her enemies. A long war meant a two-front war, then blockade, then being badly outnumbered, then the Americans. Both Ludendorff and Max Bauer made these connections in their memoirs. For Britain, a long war meant marshalling the resources of Empire more effectively, training more civilians into expert soldiers, turning more industrial effort into tanks, planes and guns. The British High Command was pre-programmed for conservatism and low risk taking, as this would be the sure way to win; the German High Command was set for higher levels of risk, as this was their only way to win.

Whilst German science and technology was often on a par with the best that the enemy could muster, production and integration of the hardware was often problematic. German steel production, manufacturing and population had all grown massively since 1870, but whether this was enough to take on the world was always highly questionable. It was also reflected in the war plans that stressed the quick ending. Industrial capacity was thus one factor, but the fact that Germany was fighting on two or more fronts at any given moment was an equally significant obstacle. A large proportion of the men enlisted were at the front, with little slack either for the factories, or for training and recuperation behind the line. The balance between new invention, production, and distribution to the troops was hard to strike effectively; shortages and the need to act on different fronts simultaneously exacerbated this situation. Not until December 1916 was the Auxiliary Service Law passed which compelled the civil population to serve the war effort, and even then this supposedly 'total mobilisation' was not enough.

German military methodology was certainly distinctive and often successful in that experimental units using a range of weapons and techniques were brought together on the battlefield at an early stage. The practicality and synergies of various combinations was thus discovered in a way that experiment in isolation could well have failed to determine. However, this apparently advanced technique fell down when it came to applying the particular to the whole. It would certainly be wrong to assume, even if we accept that the German General Staff was first to devise the best methods by means of practical experiment, that these were universally applied prior to November 1918. There were not enough light machine guns to go round, too many troops were required in the line to make universally good teaching possible, and the premature use of new elites on the battlefield killed off a proportion of the few who could have transferred their skills to the many. Those initiating the experiment had not intended that the *Sturm* battalions, and the *Sturm* platoons and companies of the existing infantry, should be an elite. The final objective was that the new methods should be taught to all to produce an all-round better army. The fact that late in the war the divisions on the Western Front had to be divided into those capable of attack and defence, and those suitable only for defence, was in fact evidence of failure. Sir Hubert Gough therefore arrived at a correct conclusion by incorrect reasoning when he suggested:

> The adoption of a system of 'star turns', of 'aces' in the air, or of 'storm troops' on the ground, may lead to some brilliant exploits, but it is a wrong system, only to be adopted by those realising their average failing strength, and it does not maintain a high average sense of duty and efficiency. Though both the French and Germans adopted the system of 'star turns' and 'storm troops' we steadily refused to follow down this path, and I am sure that we were right.

In fact the German High Command would have liked every German soldier to be a 'star turn', but logistics, casualties, and the *Erschöpfungskrieg*, or 'war of exhaustion', made sure that this could never be so. It remains to be argued whether what amounted to on-the-job training, with real bullets, was more efficient than 'schools' well behind the lines where the skills of decorated veterans could safely be taught in more forgiving environments.

Command 'by directive' rather than micromanagement often worked, but we should be wary of too great a differentiation between the major powers, since for all of them extensive preparation was critical. No significant offensive stood any serious chance of lasting effects without a strategic objective, the stockpiling of the right stores in the right place and at least an outline plan on which to commence. Perhaps the biggest single distinction of the remarkable *Angriff im Stellungskrieg*, or 'Attack in Position Warfare', was the idea that subordinates carry on until they were forced to stop, rather than be limited by their objective. This was both the great strength and the great weakness of German strategic and tactical doctrine in 1918; but then again, by this time it was indeed 'all or nothing', and this was arguably the supreme example of tactics being shaped by context.

What is very clear from the German side of the hill is that the development of the 'new tactics' was not down to any one individual. Von Hutier used the new methods in the most spectacular fashion, but the claim that he invented them is quite spurious. Bruchmüller brought together artillery tactics developed by others as well as himself, and disseminated them successfully, but perhaps only as the chosen protégé of Ludendorff. Hermann Geyer wrote well and succinctly and actively propagated the new methods through training. Less well known is that he also had a hand in the development of weapons, notably gas. General Lossberg was a convert to the new ideas which he then helped to develop. Ludendorff tried, but eventually failed, to bring the new knowledge to all, and the great offensives of 1918 did not bring victory. Wilhelm Rohr contributed much, but essentially at a battalion-experimental level. In his book *Der Grosse Krieg*, Bauer later credited Rohr and flame-thrower innovator Reddemann together with being the 'originators' of the '*Stosstrupp* idea'. This, however, was overgenerous, as elements of the new systems were invented by others, and mass implementation required overarching brains and authority.

The one name that crops up in every new field of development is that of Colonel Max Bauer himself. For, arguably, it was he who had the biggest single influence on tactics, starting with the artillery, then moving on to defence and offence. He had an important hand in the establishment of the experimental units in early 1915, and in the promotion of the knowledge that they helped to bring out. Bauer was a polymath who cultivated industrialists, sought to understand technology and attempted to apply science to tactics. An honorary doctorate from the University of Berlin marked his developmental work with heavy artillery. He also worked, less successfully, with the pioneers of chemical warfare. Feldman has gone so far as to suggest that he was 'the chief proponent' of the massive production program that Falkenhayn had demanded of the War Ministry. He dabbled in politics and army intrigue, and from 1916 had the unfailing ears of his commanders. Though the subject of political criticism in late 1917, he weathered this minor storm and learned from the experience. Ludendorff indeed once referred to him as the 'cleverest man in the army'. Even he, however, could have done little without the General Staff system, or continued favour. He also had his share of bizarre ideas, which were perhaps part of the penalty for creativity and lateral thinking. Moreover, he never claimed to have thought out all the minutiae of the new battlefield choreography personally. Bauer also sometimes regarded himself as a frustrated soldier, for though by his own account in *Der Grosse Krieg* he often spent fourteen or fifteen hours a day at the offices of the General Staff, during 'four years without rest, [his] heart was always with the troops at the front'.

It is thus very important we remember that fundamentally new minor tactics were not usually 'invented' at high level and trickled down, but often developed locally in a primitive form in response to the enemy and the vicissitudes of the battlefield. Digging deeper, spreading out, using machine guns and grenades to best advantage, and taking myriad minor initiatives were all things that appear to have started at the front in response to the heat of battle. As Ernst Jünger put it in *Das Waldchen 125* , when we find it 'too hot for us in the trench, we need no telling to take up positions in front and behind, and there we have our zone occupied in extension and depth'. Organised experiment with special units, or new doctrines, followed. Exceptions to this pattern seem to have occurred mainly with 'new' weapons such as the flame-thrower, trench mortar, and anti-tank rifle; but even with these, their improvement was usually in response to a specific demand from the front, and two of these three already existed before the war. Innovations in artillery and gas were perforce more thoroughly worked out away from the front, especially where the development of new equipments and chemicals was required, but again, many of the advances came in response to needs, and were usually tried experimentally as they were refined.

That at least some German soldiers who mattered concurred with Jünger's interpretation was confirmed when he was employed as a writer of new manuals in the inter-war period. In this context it is also worth observing that two of the most famous accounts of the infantry battle by German officers, those of Jünger and Rommel, were both exceptional, and typical of a kind. Both were involved in the critique of methods, and both were winners of the *Pour le Mérite* for conspicuous infantry actions, *Oberleutnant* Rommel's being awarded in December 1917, that of *Leutnant* Jünger in September 1918. Both would participate in the development of tactics between the wars. Perhaps most important was not their individual acts of bravery, or command, but that they were analytical about the situation in which they found themselves, and wrote well. Nevertheless, neither claimed to have 'invented' the new methods. Many others were doing similar things, less conspicuously, elsewhere. Some of the new tactical ideas certainly grew directly from the novel battlefield application of pioneer weapons that were already in use in other contexts. As Jünger pointed out:

> At the beginning of the war the pioneers had an important part to play, for their peace-time training was in any case very largely technical. So they were the first who had to do with hand bombs and mines, and from their small storm detachments sent in front of the waves of attacking troops the storm troop was evolved, that handful of resolute men who fight like a machine, each performing his own task, with the object of making a breach for the troops behind. Later, this part of their activities passed from the pioneers to the infantry, whose two radical functions of fire and movement were therefore developed to a degree that no one could have foreseen. This is another indication of the widening out of responsibility.

The idea of 'Storm', 'Shock' or 'Assault' troops acting in mutually supporting small groups, reliant upon willpower and self-motivation as much as orders, and formed in a 'storm of steel', would assume huge psychological significance. In the most stark examples, distinction would now be drawn between the unwilling and uneducated sheep of the big battalions, and those who were newly 'enlightened'. This indeed was how soldiers had been conditioned to think that it was possible to defeat an enemy superior in numbers. Formerly, orders had to be carried out and this was more than enough; now more than was ordered was the optimum. Though few could have guessed it at the time, the idea of the triumph of sheer willpower over the most monumental of obstacles would have what turned out to be the most dangerous of political resonances in Germany after 1918. Nevertheless, the parallel between the Nietzschean superman and the Stormtrooper was more than accidental. In it was found the ideal political counterweight to the 'Red Guard'.

Whilst the concept of the *Dolchstoss*, or home front 'stab in the back', betraying the 'undefeated' German army in 1918 was dubious from the outset, there is ample evidence that the *Frontschweine*, or long-suffering troops at the front, were seriously undermined in a number of ways. The history of campaigns and battles suggests, however, that this began not in October 1918, but in July 1914. Not least, the rank and file were let down by their own leaders and diplomats. Perhaps most critically, the leadership had transgressed against the most fundamental tenet of war: that of not starting any conflict which was not largely won already, off the battlefield. In this aspect, German diplomacy was disastrous. A major struggle was entered into, in which Germany lacked powerful and credible allies, stacked against a coalition which outnumbered her in population, production and potential. War planning was deficient in that it proved very difficult to deviate from a master blueprint as situations changed. In this there was a fatal departure from the ideas of Clausewitz who had long ago warned that everything was uncertain, and that even the best of plans did not usually survive contact with the enemy.

The German Navy was poorly co-ordinated with land strategy. It was supposed to be a tool to balance potential opposition and spread German influence around the globe, but it proved a significant disappointment. For though individual crews and ships fought well, and the Royal Navy's performance at Jutland was cursed with inadequate equipment, the Imperial *Kriegsmarine* was almost more of a liability than an asset. Its failure to control any life-line to the wider world was arguably irreparable, whilst ill-advised submarine warfare, despite short term benefits, only made a bad situation worse. To add insult to injury, it was not Army morale that first cracked in such an obvious way that it could no longer be ignored, but that of the Navy. The grand strategic failing of 1914 was all the more unforgivable since, with the possible exception of Britain behind her Channel moat, Germany could have expected to have defeated any one of her possible European enemies in short order.

In short, the level of risk in precipitating war in 1914 was not one which Bismarck or the older Moltke would have countenanced, and the degree of miscalculation – or arrogance – was breathtaking. What interests us here is that the consequences of the big mistakes had knock-on effects that impacted directly on the battlefields both west and east, and significantly influenced campaigns and tactical developments. Industrial shortfalls meant that choices had to be made between different types of munitions and possible production schedules. Thus it was that a conscious decision to put artillery first retarded the manufacture of tanks. Lack of tanks made the development of infantry anti-tank techniques imperative. A decision to put the maximum number of men into the field at certain junctures influenced how much could be produced to support them and re-equip them with the latest hardware. General food shortages contributed to the way in which the German army acted towards the civilians of potentially productive occupied areas. Perhaps most significantly, in entering this war, the army was set time limits on its freedom of operation, and ultimately its ability to act at all.

The impact of the new tactical ideas and their accompanying labels was highly significant on the battlefield, but in various ways the ideas associated with them would also reach into the political arena. For the Germans in particular the idea of a 'front comradeship' or 'front community' which comprised all servicemen with battle experience who looked out for one another against common enemies would prove pervasive. German war veteran societies proved politically influential in ways that the British Legion, for example, could never have imagined. Some German soldiers never really stopped being soldiers, despite Versailles and the dissolution of their units. Many joined the *Freikorps* fighting in the East, others spilled onto the streets of German towns in 1919 and 1920 ready to fight for, or against, revolution. The new language of the right wing and of polarised personal commitment took much of its vocabulary direct from the front. So it was that in 1920 when *Hauptmann* Mayr was casting about for political counterweights to the left, he seized upon the idea that 'the national workers' party', or NSDAP, would form the basis 'for a strong *Stosstrupp*'. Hitler's own bodyguard, later known to the world as the SS, started life as the *Stosstrupp* Adolf Hitler. His book, which had begun as the clumsily titled *Four and a Half Years of Struggle Against Lies, Stupidity and Cowardice*, found fame or infamy as *Mein Kampf*, literally 'my battle' or 'my struggle'. The term 'front' was applied to many and various things including political groupings and workers associations. The paramilitaries of 'the movement' were no mere 'guards' but the 'Storm Detachment': the *Sturm Abteilung*, or SA.

After some wars new methods are forgotten, and have to be painfully relearned at a later date. In the case of Germany and the new infantry tactics in 1918 this was not the case – perhaps surprisingly given the apparent discontinuities between the massive army of the last Kaiser, and the tiny force of the new *Reichswehr* constricted by the proscriptions of the Versailles treaty. The new field service regulations issued under the auspices of General Hans von Seeckt in 1921 made this abundantly clear. The theoretical basis of all action was that 'from the mission and the situation' commanders would make their decisions. What would finally bring victory was attack:

> The attack alone dictates the law to the enemy. The superiority of leader and troops comes best into play here. Especially effective is the envelopment of one or both flanks and the attack in the enemy's rear. In this way the enemy can be destroyed. All orders for the attack must bear the stamp of great decisiveness. The leader's will to victory must be shared down to the last man.

Another less clearly articulated aspiration was to avoid the circumstances under which protracted trench warfare might again arise. Training stressed more open environments, use of terrain, and close co-operation of support weapons – not drills for 'chewing through' deep defensive zones. Co-ordination with artillery was critical, but not at the expense of allowing battles to deteriorate into lengthy set-piece actions and losing both opportunity and initiative. Doubtless this was partly ideological, but it was also hugely practical, as a small army was ill equipped for such large and protracted operations. Similarly stressed was the idea of the 'delaying defence'; something which might well be required when faced by a much larger enemy.

The composition of rifle squads and small-unit tactics were also addressed in 1921, and the latest organisation was clearly based on the experience of 1918. Squads were now to be of eight men, who might operate in a skirmish line, extended file or indeed any formation dictated by the needs of the moment. On the ability and determination of the leader hinged the fate of the squad. Squads might be combined not only into regulation platoons (*Zugen*) but small 'battle groups' (*Kampfgruppen*) with at least one machine gun and other weapons. In 1922 the *Ausbildungsvorschift für die Infanterie*, or infantry training regulations, fully accepted the permanent integration of light machine guns, which were now to be arranged on the basis of a 'rifle troop' and 'machine gun troop' working together within every *Gruppe* or squad. With time the distinction between the rifle and machine gun sub-sections would be progressively eroded, so by the late 1930s the standard squad was ten men: the leader and a deputy; three men for the light machine gun; and five riflemen. As manuals such as Dr Reibert's *Der Dienst Unterricht im Heere*, Major Bodo Zimmermann's *Die Neue Gruppe*, and *Der Feuerkampf der Schützenkompanie* (1940) make clear, the full tactical integration of machine weapons, sought in 1918 but never fully achieved, was now orthodoxy. Few if any German officers would attempt to micromanage the activity of a whole platoon or company in action: initiative on the tactical detail of positions, camouflage, field craft, and other matters rested squarely with the individual and his squad leader. More senior ranks would only be likely to intervene to initiate a task, or to correct a serious omission.

To this extent the old *Stoss* and Stormtroop ideas of World War I made possible the infantry contribution to the *Blitzkrieg* of 1940. Indirectly, they also assisted in the evolution of the tactics of other arms, such as those of the parachutists and other special forces.

However, what they obviously could not do was add very much to the development of tactics for armour or aircraft. *The Attack in Position Warfare* had had relatively little to say about the detailed co-operation of infantry and aircraft, and virtually nothing about the role of the tank. Infantry-to-air communication had been in its infancy in 1918, to put it kindly, and the German failure to field a meaningful tank arm in the Great War is obvious. These crucial elements of what we now recognise as mechanised warfare had to be developed, implemented and learned between the wars, though it is not often appreciated how quickly this process was begun. The use of civilian lorries as troop transport in official training was certainly under way as early as 1921, and aircraft and other technological weapons, completely banned to the German military by Versailles, were openly featured by proxy during the manoeuvres of 1924. During these exercises dummy tanks and anti-tank guns were used, and officers rode around on specially marked motorcycles simulating reconnaissance aircraft. When rearmament brought new weapons in the mid 1930s they were not therefore presented to a completely naive and unpractised Wehrmacht, but to troops who already had begun to learn the rudiments of how they might be operated in battle.

Interestingly, after the First World War, the Reichswehr, and later the Wehrmacht, initially preferred the word *Stoss* (also rendered as '*Stoß*' in twentieth-century German), meaning 'shock', 'push' or 'thrust', to the word *Sturm* meaning 'storm' or 'assault'. As late as 1939 'shock troops' was the usual army terminology and *Sturm* was left more to party and political usage until about that time. If this was a conscious act of separation on the part of professional soldiers it was eventually broken down, for *Sturm* was again applied to units and weapons as the Second World War progressed. In this context it is significant to note that the title of Jünger's famous book *Storm of Steel* was actually mistranslated: he did not write a book with its inspiration 'from the Diary of a Storm Troop officer', but *Aus dem Tagebuch eines Stosstruppfuhrers*, 'from the Diary of a Shock Troop Leader'. The assumption that the 'Stormtrooper' was the root of what was new and somehow in a different category to the tactics which had produced him was now thoroughly absorbed, both into the German psyche, and into the English language. The legend would prove powerful and enduring.

Appendix I

DATES OF INTRODUCTION OF COMBAT WEAPONS AND EQUIPMENT TO A TYPICAL GERMAN INFANTRY REGIMENT, 1914–1918

Pre-War Rifle; Bayonet; Machine guns (six in MG Company); P08 and other Pistols (for specialists and officers); personal small spade for entrenching; swords (officers and senior NCOs); grenades available in very small quantities, usually in the hands of attached Pioneer personnel only

December 1914 Hand grenades general issue

January 1915 Telescopic sights for selected snipers

February 1915 Rifle grenades
Pioneer companies deploy six *Minenwerfer* each (initially not part of the infantry regiment, but used in supporting role)

April 1915 Additional shields for machine guns

August 1915 Order for replacement of swords with bayonets - though most officers and senior NCOs had ceased to take swords to the trenches already.

December 1915 Issue of effective, universal-model gas mask, supplanting temporary expedient types

August 1916 Machine gun strength reaches 15 with regiment (gradual increase from pre-war establishment)
Completion of steel helmet issue

September 1916 Regiment's machine guns now organised in three companies of six weapons (total 18 MGs)

February 1917 Deployment of twenty-four *Granatenwerfer* with regiment (rodded-type rifle grenades discontinued)
Deployment of twelve new light *Minenwerfer* with regiment (four per battalion intended to replace whatever models were previously in use)

April 1917 Light machine guns (four per regiment)
Telescopic sights rationalised at three per company (approximately twelve per battalion, thirty-six per regiment)

May 1917 Light machine guns sufficient for two per company (approximately eight per battalion, twenty-four per regiment)

August 1917 *Granatenwerfer* reorganised as two per company

September 1917   Light machine guns now four per company (total of approximately forty-eight with regiment) possible for individual platoons to use integrated weapons for close support

December 1917   Formation of dedicated signals section integral to regiment

February 1918   Light machine guns now six per company (seventy-two in regiment) machine weapons now sufficient to use within *Korporalshaft* or even squads (*Gruppe*).

March 1918   Individual signal sections for each battalion, and regimental staff

Mid 1918   First appearance of small numbers of anti tank rifles and sub machine guns with front line units

September 1918   *Minenwerfer* reorganised into regimental company

Appendix II

BASIC INFANTRY REGIMENT STRUCTURE, AUGUST 1914

Regimental Staff
4 officers (Commanding Officer, Adjutant, Medical Officer and Transport Officer)
49 NCOs and other ranks including bandsmen

Three Battalions, Each Comprising
1 Battalion Commander
4 Rifle Company Commanders
18 Lieutenants to include medical officers, supply officers and paymaster
1,054 NCOs and other ranks.

Each of the Twelve Rifle Companies of the Regiment Being
5 officers
259 other ranks (each company being subdivided into three platoons; each platoon into four sub sections or *Korporalshaft* ; each half platoon into two squads or *Gruppe*)

The Machine Gun or '13th' Company
1 Company Commander
3 Lieutenants
133 NCOs and other ranks
6 MGs

Major Changes up to 1918
Whilst weapons were increased, manpower generally decreased, battalion book-strengths being commonly about 800 by 1917 (regiments therefore fielding an average of about 2,500 against approximately 3,500 at the start of the war). In the last weeks of the war it was intended to reduce the number of basic rifle companies in each regiment from twelve to nine.

With the increasing numbers of heavy machine guns during 1915 and early 1916, machine gun companies were strengthened, separate units formed and then increased to two per regiment. By the end of 1916 there were usually three MG companies per regiment (one for each battalion). The slowness of light machine guns to be deployed is reflected in the fact that although an issue of three per company was decreed as early as December 1916, many units did not manage this level of deployment until mid-1917. Regimental signal sections were formed in 1917, and regimental *Minenwerfer* companies were formed in 1918.

Bibliography

Anon. *Anleitung zur Langen Pistole 08 mit Ansteckbarem Trommelmagazin*, 1917.

Anon. *Merkblatt Für Tankbekampfung*. German 2nd Army, 27 January, 1918.

Aron, R. *Clausewitz, Philosopher of War*. New York, 1986.

Ashworth, T. *Trench Warfare*. London, 1980.

Atteridge, A.H. *The German Army at War*. London, 1915.

Barnett, C. *The Swordbearers: Studies in Supreme Command in the First World War*. London, 1963.

Barnett, C. et al. *Old Battles and New Defences: Can We Learn From Military History?* London, 1986.

Bauer, M. *Der Grosse Krieg in Feld und Heimat, Erinnerung und Betrachtungen*. Tubingen, 1921.

Behr, F.J. (trans) *Drill Regulations for the Infantry, German Army, 1906*. Translated for the General Staff, US Army, Washington, 1907.

Berghahn, V.R. *Germany and the Approach of War in 1914*. London, 1973.

Bloch, I.S. *Modern Weapons and Modern War*. London, 1899.

Bloem, W. *The Advance From Mons, 1914: The Experiences of a German Infantry Officer*. Leipzig, 1916. Translated by G.C. Wynne and reproduced Solihull, 2004.

Brown, M. *The Imperial War Museum Book of 1918, Year of Victory*. London, 1998.

Brown, M. *Verdun*. Stroud, 2000.

Brose, E.D. *The Kaiser's Army: The Politics of Military Technolgy in Germany During the Machine Age, 1870–1918*. Oxford, 2001.

Bruce, R. *Machine Guns of World War I*. London, 1997.

Buchner, A. *Der Minenkrieg Auf Vauquois*. Karsfeld, 1982.

Bull, S. *Stormtrooper*. London, 1999.

Bull, S. *World War I Trench Warfare*. Oxford, 2002.

Carr, W. *A History of Germany, 1815–1945*. 2nd edition. London, 1972.

Chickering, R. *Imperial Germany and the Great War, 1914–1918*. 2nd edition. Cambridge, 2004.

Citino, R.M. *The Path to Blitzkrieg: Doctrine and Training in the German Army, 1920–1939*. Boulder, 1999.

Clark, A. *The Eastern Front 1914–1918*. London, 1971.

Cron, H. *Geschichte des Deutschen Heeres im Welkrieg 1914-1918*. Berlin, 1937.

Dane, E. *Trench Warfare:The Effects of Spade Power in Modern Battles*. London, 1915.

Dean, B. *Helmets and Body Armour in Modern Warfare*. New Haven, 1930.

Drury, I. *German Stormtrooper, 1914–1918*. London, 1995.

Duffy, C. *Through German Eyes: The British and the Somme*. London, 2006.

Ebelshauser, G.A. *The Passage: A Tragedy of the First World War*. Huntingdon, USA, 1984.

Edkins, D. *The Prussian Orden Pour le Merite: History of the Blue Max*. Falls Church, 1981.

Ellis, J. *The Social History of the Machine Gun*. 3rd edition. London, 1987.

Engen, R. 'Steel Against Fire: The Bayonet in the First World War', in *Journal of Military and Strategic Studies*, Spring 2006, Volume 8: Issue 3.

English, J.A. *A Perspective on Infantry*. New York, 1981.

von Falkenhayn, E. *General Headquarters, 1914–1916, and its Critical Decisions*. Berlin and London, 1919.

Feldman, G.D. *Army, Industry and Labor in Germany, 1914–1918*. Princeton, 1966; reprinted with new foreword, Providence and Oxford, 1992.

Fleischer, W. *German Trench Mortars and Infantry Mortars 1914-1945*. Atglen, 1996.

Foch, F. et al. *The Two Battles of the Marne*. London, 1927.

Foerster, W. *Wir Kämpfer im Weltkrieg: Feldzugsbriefe und Kriegstagebücher von Frontkämpfern Aus dem Material des Reichsarchivs*. Berlin, 1929.

Franke, H. *Handbuch der Neuzeitlichen Wehrwissenschaften*. Berlin, 1937.

General Staff (UK). *Reports on the Subject of German 'Flammenwerfer'*. 1915. Translated by the General Staff, SS 71.

General Staff (UK). *Notes on German Artillery Emplacements, 1915*. Translated from the French, 1916.

General Staff (UK). Translation of a German Document: *Experiences Gained in the Winter Battle in Champagne From the Point of View of the Organisation of the Enemy's Lines of Defence and the Means of Combating an Attempt to Pierce Our Line*. Reprinted as CDS 303, 1915.

General Staff (UK). *A Study of the Attack in the Present Phase of War: Impressions and Reflections of a Company Commander*. Translated from the French as CDS 333.

General Staff (UK). *Translation of a German Document: Proposals for the Technical Methods to be Adopted in an Attempt to Break Through a Strongly Fortified Position, Based on Errors Which Appear to Have Been Committed by the French*. Reprinted as CDS 304, 1915.

General Staff (UK). *Translation of a German Document: Essential Principles for the Defence of Positions*. Reprinted as SS 471, 1915.

General Staff (UK). *Notes on German Army Corps. XIV Reserve Corps and 52nd Division*. SS 394, March 1916.

General Staff (UK). *Translation of a German Document: German Raid on the British Trenches Near La Boiselle, 11 April 1916*. Reprinted as SS 462.

General Staff (UK). *Manual of Position Warfare for All Arms, Part I, the Construction of Field Positions (Stellungsbau). Issued by the Prussian War Ministry, Berlin, 1916.* Translated and reproduced, May 1917.

General Staff (UK). *Flammenwerfer*. Translation of German Document 26655, 20/4/16.

General Staff (UK). *Notes on German Army Corps. IX Reserve Corps*. SS 424, May 1916.

General Staff (UK). *Extracts from German Documents and Correspondence*. SS 473, 1916.

General Staff (UK). *Duties and Employment of the 4th Artillery Survey Section (Artillerie-Messtrupp) and the 49th Sound Ranging Section (Schallmesstrupp)*. Translation of a German document. Reprinted as SS 447, 18 April 1916.

General Staff (UK). *German Instructions Regarding Gas Warfare*. Translation of a German Pamphlet Captured in July 1916. Reprinted as SS 449.

General Staff (UK). *Translation of a German Document: German Mining Officer's Diary Captured at Fricourt, July 1916*. Reprinted as SS 460.

General Staff (UK). *Extract from Old Mining Regulations, Issued by the general of Pioneers, Army HQ Laon, April 1915.* Translated from a German Pamphlet Captured at Fricourt, July 1916.

General Staff (UK). *Translation of a German document: Experiences of the IV German Corps in the Battle of the Somme, During July, 1916.* Reprinted as SS 478.

General Staff (UK). *Translation of a German Document: Experiences Gained from the September Offensives on the Fronts of the Sixth and Third Armies.* Reprinted as SS 454, July 1916.

General Staff (UK). *Translation of a German Document: Regulations for Machine Gun Officers and Non Commissioned Officers,* 1916.

General Staff (UK). *Translation of a German Document: Order of the 6th Bavarian Division Regarding Machine Guns,* 3 September, 1916. Reprinted as SS 487.

General Staff (UK). *Translation of a German Document: Lessons Drawn from the Battle of the Somme by Stein's Group.* Reprinted as SS 480, October 1916.

General Staff (UK). *German Instructions for the Employment of Granatenwerfer or Stick Bomb Throwers.* October 1916, reprinted as SS541, 1917.

General Staff (UK). *Translation of a German Document: German Instructions for the Employment of Flame Projectors.* Issued by the Chief of the General Staff of the Field Army, 12 December, 1915. Reprinted as SS 531, December 1916.

General Staff (UK). *Summary of Recent Information Regarding the German Army and its Methods.* January 1917, SS 537.

General Sraff (UK). *The 1916 Pattern Bomb Thrower (Granatenwerfer 16).* SS546, March 1917.

General Staff (UK). Abbreviated Translation of a German Document: *Weapons of Close Combat (Nahkampfmittel) 1 January 1917.* Issued by the Chief of Staff of the Field Army, Berlin, 1917; General Staff (Intelligence) 23/5/17, SS 562.

General Staff (UK). *Extracts No.4 From German Documents and Correspondence.* Reprinted as SS 532, 1917.

General Staff (UK). *Effect on Enemy of Our gas Attacks.* Third Report, 1917, SS 138/3.

General Staff (UK). *Notes on German Shells.* 2nd edition. May, 1918.

General Staff (UK). *Machine Gun Notes, incorporating the German Machine Gunners' Catechism,* July 1918, SS 201/3.

General Staff (UK). *Notes on the 08 (Heavy) and 08/15 (Light) German Machine Guns.* August 1918.

General Staff (UK). *Translation of a German Document: Manual of Position Warfare For All Arms, Part 14 Provisional, The Attack in Position Warfare, 1 January 1918, with Amendments 26/1/18 and 27/7/18.* Reprinted 11 October 1918.

General Staff (UK). *The German Tank 'Elfriede'.* SS 714, 1 June 1918.

Goldsmith, D.L. *The Devil's Paintbrush.* Toronto, 1989.

Goodspeed, D.J. *Ludendorff.* London, 1966.

Gough, H. *The Fifth Army.* London, 1931.

Griffith, P. *Forward into Battle: Fighting Tactics From Waterloo to Vietnam.* Chichester, 1981.

Griffith, P. *Battle Tactics of the Western Front.* Yale, 1994.

Griffith, P. *Fortifications of the Western Front.* Oxford, 2004.

Gudmundsson, B.I. *Stormtroop Tactics: Innovation in the German Army, 1914–1918.* New York, 1989.

Haber, L.F. *The Poisonous Cloud.* Oxford, 1986.

Hajny V. and A.V. Petricek. *Der Grosse Krieg: Fotografien Tschechischer und Mahrischer Museen.* Brno, 2004.

Herwig, H.H. *The First World War: Germany and Austria-Hungary, 1914–1918.* London, 1997.

Herwig, H.H. *Operation Michael: The Last Card*. University of Calgary, (Web Published) undated.

Hicks, J.E. *German Weapons, Uniforms, Insignia, 1841–1918*. La Canada, 1958.

von Hindenburg, P. *Out of My Life*. Trans. F.A. Holt. London, 1920.

Horne, A. *The Price of Glory: Verdun 1916*. New York, 1962.

Howard, M. *Clausewitz*. Oxford, 1983.

Jackson, G.W. *'Unofficial' Diagrams of German Grenades, 1917: Egg; Rifle 1913 &1914; Disc; Cylindrical Stick; Ball; Rocket for Granatenwerfer*.

Joffre, J. et al. *The Two Battles of the Marne*. London, 1937.

Jünger, E. *The Storm of Steel*. 1929. Reproduced with an introduction by P. Griffith, London 1994.

Jünger, E. *Das Wäldchen 125*. Translated as *Copse 125*, and reprinted 1985.

Kaltenegger, R. *Die Geschichte der Deutschen Gebirgstruppe 1915 bis Heute*. Stuttgart, 1980.

Kaufmann, S. 'Raumrevolution. Die Militarishen Raumffassungen Zwischen Ersten und Zweitem Weltkrieg', in *Der Weltkrieg 1914-1918*. Berlin 2004.

Klein, F. et al. *Deutschland im Ersten Weltkrieg*. Three vols, Berlin, 1968–1969.

Koch, F. *Flamethrowers of the German Army 1914–1945*. Atglen, 1997.

Lavisse, E.C. *Field Equipment of the European Foot Soldier*. 1902. Reprinted Nashville, 1994.

Linder, A.P. *Princes of the Trenches: Narrating the German Experience of the First World War*. Columbia, 1996.

Linnenkohl, H. *Vom Einzelschuss Zur Feuerwalze: Der Wettlauf Zwischen Technik und Taktik im Ersten Weltkrieg*. Koblenz, 1990.

Ludendorff, E. *Meine Kriegserinnerungen*. Berlin, 1919. (Translated as *My War Memories, 1914–1918*. London, 1919).

Lupfer, T.T. *The Dynamics of Doctrine: The Change in German Tactical Doctrine During the First World War*. Leavenworth Paper, 4, Combat Studies Institute, July 1981.

Marshall, G.C. et al. *Infantry in Battle*. 3rd edition. Washington DC, 1939.

Marshall, S.L.A. *Men Against Fire: The Problem of Battle Command*. New York, 1947. Reproduced with an introduction by R.W. Glenn, University of Oklahoma, 2000.

von Merkatz, F. *Unterrichtsbuch Für Die Maschinengewehr-Kompagnien, Gerat 08*. Berlin, 1907. New edition 1917.

Middlebrook, M. *The Kaiser's Battle, 21 March 1918: The First Day of the German Spring Offensive*. London, 1978.

Mott, T.B. (trans). *The Memoirs of Marshal Foch*. London, 1931.

Moyer, L.V. *Victory Must be Ours: The German Army in the Great War, 1914–1918*. New York, 1995.

Nash, D. *German Artillery, 1914–1918*. London, 1970.

Nash, D. (ed). *German Army Handbook, 1918*. General Staff, 1918; reproduced with a new introduction, London, 1977.

Nash, D. *Imperial German Army Handbook, 1914–1918*. London, 1980.

Nevin, T. *Ernst Jünger and Germany*. Duke University, 1996.

Oldham, P. *Pill Boxes on the Western Front*. London, 1995.

Ousby, I. *The Road to Verdun*. London, 2002.

Paschall, R. *The Defeat of Imperial Germany, 1917–1918*. Chapel Hill, 1989.

Passingham, I. *All the Kaiser's Men*. Stroud, 2003.

Pitt, B. *1918: The Last Act*. London, 1962.

Pollard, A.W. (ed). *Subject Index of the Books Relating to the European War, 1914–1918, Acquired by the British Museum, 1914-1920*. London, 1922. Reproduced London, 1966.

Rawling, B. *Surviving Trench Warfare: Technology and the Canadian Corps, 1914–1918.* Toronto, 1992.

Renn, L. *War.* London, 1929. (Fictionalised account of A.F.V. von Golssenau)

Robert, Capt. *I Have Captured a Boche Machine Gun... What Can I Do With It?* Paris, 1918.

Rommel, E. *Infanterie Greift An.* Potsdam,1937: English translation with a new introduction by M. Rommel, London, 1990.

Rosinski, H. *The German Army.* English reprint, ed. G.A. Craig. London, 1966.

Samuels, M. *Doctrine and Dogma: German and British Infantry Tactics in the First World War.* New York, 1992.

Samuels, M. *Command or Control? Command, Training and Tactics in the British and German Armies, 1888–1918.* London, 1995.

Saunders, A. *Weapons of the Trench War, 1914–1918.* Stroud, 1999.

Sava, G. *School For War.* London, 1942.

Sheldon, J. *The German Army on the Somme, 1914–1916.* Barnsley, 2005.

Stackpole, P.T. *German Tactics in the Michael Offensive.* Unpublished, West Point, 1981.

Stone, N. *The Eastern Front, 1914–1917.* London, 1975.

Storch, S. *Vom Feldgrauen Buchhandler: Stimmungsbilder Briefe und Karten.* Magdeburg, 1915.

Sulzbach, H. *Zwei Lebende Mauern.* 1935. Translated with a new foreword as *With the German Guns:Four Years on the Western Front.* London, 1998.

Sweet, F.W. *Evolution of Infantry Assault Tactics 1850–1918.* American Military University, (Web Published) 1997.

Szczepanski, M. *Erinnerungsblatter Aus Der Geschichte Des Fusilier Regiments Generalfeldmarschall Prinz Albrecht von Preussen (Hann.) Nr 73.* Berlin, 1923.

Trutnovsky, F. *Zbrane Pechoty – Rucini a Puskove Granaty.* Czechoslovakia, 1921.

Walter, J. *The German Rifle.* London, 1979.

Walter, J. *The Luger Book.* London, 1986.

War Department (US). *Histories of Two Hundred and Fifty-One Divisions of the German Army Which Participated in the War.* Chaumont, 1919. Reprinted with a new introduction, London, 1989.

War Ministry (German). *DVE. Nr 275: Feld-Pioneerdienst aller Waffen.* Berlin, 1911.

War Office (UK). *The German Forces in the Field, 7th Revision, 11th November, 1918.* Reproduced Nashville, 1995.

Werth, G. *Verdun: Die Schlacht und Der Mythos.* Bergish Gladbach, 1979.

Winteringham T. and J.N. Blashford-Snell. *Weapons and Tactics.* London, 1973.

Witkop, P (ed). *German Students' War Letters.* 1929. English translation with a new introduction by J. Winter, University of Pennsylvania, 2002.

Zabecki, D.T. *Steel Wind: Colonel Georg Bruchmüller and the Birth of Modern Artillery.* Westport, 1994.

Ziemann, D. *Denkmalprojekt: Verlustlisten.* Web published, 2006.

Index

If you enjoyed this book, you may also be interested in…

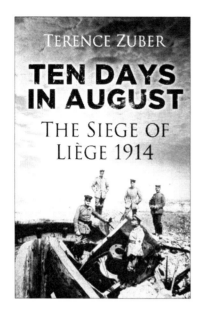

Ten Days in August
The Siege of Liège 1914

TERRENCE ZUBER

978 0 7524 9144 8

In August 1914 the German main attack was conducted by the 2nd Army. It had the missions of taking the vital fortresses of Liège and Namur, and then defeating the Anglo-French-Belgian forces in the open plains of northern Belgium.

The German attack on the Belgian fortress at Liège from 5 to 16 August 1914 had tremendous political and military importance. Nevertheless, there has never been a complete account of the siege. The German and Belgian sources are fragmentary and biased. The short descriptions in English are general, use few Belgian sources, and are filled with inaccuracies. Making use of both German and Belgian sources, this book for the first time describes and evaluates the construction of the fortress, its military purpose, the German plan, and the conduct of the German attack. Previous accounts emphasise the importance of the huge German "Big Bertha" cannon, to the virtual exclusion of everything else: *Ten Days in August* shows that the effect of this gun was a myth, and shows how the Germans really took the fortress.

This is how the whole bloody mess started.

Visit our website and discover thousands of other History Press books.

www.thehistorypress.co.uk

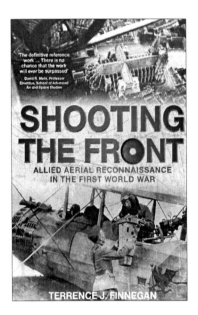

Shooting the Front

TERRENCE J. FINNEGAN

978 0 7524 9954 3

The First World War demanded revolutionary technology to break the vicious stalemate in which the armies of Europe found themselves as soon as static warfare became established. In the critical world of military intelligence, aviation assumed a vital role through aerial reconnaissance in reinforcing successful decision-making. The demands of warfare not only spurred aviationâ s development, it led to technological advances in aerial photography, radio intercepts, acoustics and optics that became the foundation for intelligence throughout the twentieth century and to the present day. Colonel Terry Finneganâ s Shooting the Front reviews the entire evolution of Allied aerial photography and photographic interpretation during the Great War, in a text packed with data and based upon meticulous research in archives worldwide. The photographs included are both informative and spectacular, charting perforce the early years of aviation itself. Shooting the Front shows not only how important aerial reconnaissance was to the war effort, but also how it became the foundation for modern-day exploitation of imagery and geospatial intelligence used to guide todayâ s decision makers on global issues, and shaped intelligence work for generations to come.

Visit our website and discover thousands of other History Press books.

www.thehistorypress.co.uk

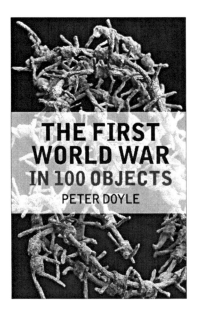

The First World War in 100 Objects

PETER DOYLE

978 0 7524 8811 0

Objects allow us to reach out and touch the past and they play a living role in history today. Through them we can understand the experience of men and women during the First World War. They bear witness to the stories of men whose only morning comfort in the trenches was the rum ration, children who grew up with only one photograph of the father that they would never get to know, women who would sacrifice their girlhood in hospitals yards from the frontline, pinning a brooch on to remind themselves of a past life. Weapons like the machine gun and vehicles like the tank that transformed the battlefield; planes that had barely learnt to be flown entangled in dogfights far above the barbed wire of the frontline; German submarines that stalked shipping across the seas. Through these incredible artefacts, Peter Doyle tells the story of the First World War in a whole new light.

Visit our website and discover thousands of other History Press books.

www.thehistorypress.co.uk